The Medway and the Military

Mel Swain

ISBNs:
Paperback 978-1-80227-382-3
eBook 978-1-80227-383-0

Mel was born and raised in Gillingham (Kent). An Open University
graduate who trained as a teacher in Brighton, he has lived in Sussex
ever since and taught in several comprehensive schools.

Contents

Chapter 1

The River Medway

"And, the truth is, I do fear so much that the whole kingdom is undone."

That was what Samuel Pepys (1633-1703) wrote in his diary on 12 June 1667. Pepys worked for the navy, but he is best remembered for his personal accounts of what happened in England in the 1660s. So what was he writing about here that provoked such a dramatic comment? Was it the restoration of the Stuarts, one of whom had caused the English Civil War? No. Was it the Great Plague? No. Was it the Great Fire of London? No.

The past is unalterable, but history (the record of the past) is not set in stone. In 'History the Betrayer', E.H.Dance (p.21) tells us how "each people tends to recall and record the things which are congenial to itself, and to forget or ignore those which are favourable to foreigners". Significant victories such as Agincourt in 1415, the defeat of the Spanish Armada in 1588 (overlooking the fact that the weather had a lot to do with it), Trafalgar in 1805 and Waterloo in 1815 are well documented and widely known about in the UK. Even some defeats, such as Dunkirk in 1940, are spun as success stories. However, ignominious failures such as the Dutch raid on the Medway (the chief river of Kent) in 1667 - which Pepys was writing about - receive much less recognition. The second Anglo-Dutch War began in 1665, and the Dutch raid on the dockyards in the Medway was a humiliation (13 English ships were sunk, burned or captured, with no Dutch losses), and it showed that the English could not defend their own coastline at that point in time.

That was not the first time that the River Medway had been the scene of a defeat for the home team. The Battle of the Medway took place in 43 CE and was the first major recorded encounter of the Roman invasion of Britain under the orders of Claudius, the fourth Roman emperor. The battle took place in the lands of the Iron Age tribe of the Cantiaci, possibly at Rochester, where there was a large settlement at that time. It lasted nearly two days.

Not every foreign incursion up the Medway was successful. During the eighth century, the east coast of Britain was under constant attack from Vikings, and the river became a popular route for the invaders to use. However, when Vikings tried to capture Rochester in 883, local citizens fought them off until Alfred the Great and his Saxon army arrived.

The Jutes had earlier occupied the east of Kent, while the Saxons lived to the west. That provides at least one of the theories as to how the now rather pointless distinction between 'Men of Kent' (people born to the south of the River Medway) and 'Kentish Men' (those born to the north or west of the river) came about; females would be called 'Maids'. Another theory is that it marked the division of Kent into two dioceses (Canterbury and Rochester) from the year 604.

A man named Edmund Spenser worked as secretary to the

Bishop of Rochester in 1589 when he was writing 'The Faerie Queene', one of the longest poems in the English language, consisting of more than 36,000 lines in six books. It is mainly an allegorical work for which Elizabeth I gave Spenser a pension of £50 a year for life, although there is no evidence that she read any of it. In the fourth book, Spenser describes the 'marriage' of the Thames and the Medway in some detail.

The River Medway, where Francis Drake learned to sail, is one of the longest rivers in the south east of England. It begins its 70-mile journey to the Thames Estuary from a spring in Butcher's Wood in Turner's Hill in West Sussex, a village situated between Crawley and East Grinstead. Turner's Hill stands on a steep ridge line at one of the highest points (580 feet above sea level) of the Weald. 13 miles of the river are in West or East Sussex, the remainder of it is in Kent. It initially flows in an easterly direction, but it then turns northwards and continues through a gap in the North Downs. It enters the Thames Estuary in a 1.5 mile space between the Isle of Grain and Sheerness on the Isle of Sheppey.

The Medway and its tributaries flow through mainly rural areas, including small villages such as Forest Row and Hartfield; the latter was where A.A.Milne, the author of the 'Winnie the Pooh' books, lived in a farmhouse and from where many of his stories are set. That house was later owned by Brian Jones, the founder of the Rolling Stones, who was found dead in its swimming pool in 1969.

The middle section of the Medway is fed by six tributaries – the Eden, Bourne, Teise, Beult, Loose and Len – which has always made the area vulnerable to serious flooding. Near Wateringbury there is a triple confluence of the Beult and the Teise with the Medway. The Leigh Barrier was constructed in 1981 to hold back the river at high flows, allowing water to be fed through at a controlled rate. There are eleven locks on the river.

The village of Penshurst is located at the confluence of the Medway with the Eden. In the centre of the village is Penshurst Place, which was built in 1341. Henry VIII took possession of it during the latter part of his reign, and his son Edward VI gave it to Sir William Sidney in 1552. It has been owned by the Sidney family ever since.

Yalding has the longest surviving medieval bridge in Kent. It is made of Kentish ragstone and crosses the Beult, which is the main tributary of the Medway. The 450-foot bridge dates from at least the 15th century, and it was probably built on the site of an earlier wooden bridge. It was widened in 1848.

There are five towns on the River Medway, and as you head downstream the first of those is Tonbridge, from where since 1746 the river has been navigable to the Thames Estuary because of improvements to the channel. That allowed materials such as coal and lime to be transported to Tonbridge, and for gunpowder, hops and timber to be carried down river to Maidstone (the second town on the river) and the Thames. Before that date, the river was not navigable above Maidstone.

A motte and bailey castle was built in Tonbridge towards the end of the 11th century. That was a stone keep on a raised area of ground, accompanied by a walled courtyard and surrounded by a protective ditch and fence. It was built to replace the original wooden keep which burnt down in 1088. The arrow which killed William II (Rufus) in 1100 was shot by Walter Tirel, who was born in Tonbridge. The town has a famous public school which was established in 1552 to educate the sons of the local gentry and farmers.

The UK's first speeding fine was issued by Tonbridge magistrates in 1896, and it cost the driver of a Benz car one shilling for doing 8mph in a 2mph zone in the village of Paddock Wood. He was apprehended by a policeman who had given chase – on his bicycle! Tonbridge was the location of a much more serious crime in 2006; the largest cash theft in British criminal history occurred at the Securitas depot there.

In 1943, during World War II, flyer Hector MacCourt of Bidborough near Tonbridge was shot down in German-occupied territory near Arnhem in the Netherlands. While he was hiding in the woods, a 14-year- old girl who could speak English took him some food, as she had done for other downed flyers. She noticed that he had his family's gold signet ring with him, warned him that the Germans would take it if he was captured, and persuaded him to let her look after it until the war was over. He was captured, but in 1946 she kept her promise to return it and tracked him down in Bidborough. Her name was Audrey Ruston, but most people will remember her as the actress and humanitarian Audrey Hepburn (1929-1993).

MacCourt died at the age of 30 in 1952 from poliomyelitis, a disease which may well have plagued humans for thousands of years. It probably still would if anti-vaxxers had prevailed, but polio was eliminated from the Western hemisphere by 1994 because of widespread vaccination, and it now only exists in small pockets of Asia.

Maidstone, which is 25 miles from the mouth of the River Medway, is the county town of Kent. There is evidence of settlement in the area dating back before the Stone Age, and it features in the Domesday Book as 'Meddestane'. In the 14th century, a rebel priest called John Ball was imprisoned there and was freed by Kentish rebels under the command of Wat Tyler (who is thought to have lived in the town) during the Peasants' Revolt of 1381.

The Battle of Maidstone of 1648 occurred towards the end of the English Civil War and was won by the Parliamentarians. Andrew Broughton, the mayor of Maidstone, was also the clerk to the High Court of Justice, and he was responsible for declaring the death sentence on Charles I in January 1649. When Charles II, who is sometimes and inappropriately referred to as 'the merry monarch', became king in 1660, savage reprisals were taken against those associated with his father's death, but Broughton escaped to Switzerland and stayed there for the rest of his life.

The men's prison in Maidstone is one of the oldest penal institutions in Britain, having been in operation since 1819. The notorious gangster Reggie Kray was married in there in 1997.

A permanent military presence was established in Maidstone in 1798 as part of the British response to the threat of the French Revolution. Maidstone Barracks (now known as Invicta Park) was a major cavalry barracks at a stationing point between London and the Kent coast. It is now home to a part of the Corps of Royal Engineers.

The Medway has played a major role in Kentish history for centuries. When hops were introduced from the mainland of Europe in the 16th century, the Medway provided water to make Maidstone the centre of the Kentish brewing industry. Barges would carry out cargoes of stone and timber, and later iron, paper and fruit (particularly cherries), especially after navigation on the river was improved in the 1740s. It would be used to bring in butter and cheese from East Anglia, coal from the north of England, softwood from the Baltic, and cheese and tiles from the Netherlands. The coming of railway and road transport reduced the commercial importance of the river, although cement was manufactured using chalk and Medway clay from the mid 19th century. Today the river is mainly used for sport and leisure activities.

During World War II, the underwater oil pipeline, codenamed 'Operation Pluto', was developed in order to support the planned Allied invasion of mainland Europe. A prototype pipe was first tested in May 1942, when a line was run under the River Medway.

Apart from Tonbridge and Maidstone, there are three other towns on the river. These are Rochester, Chatham and Gillingham which, along with Strood and Rainham, are known collectively as 'The Medway Towns'. Between them they had a total population of 278,016 in 2019.

Chapter 2

The Medway Towns

Daniel Defoe (1660-1731), who is most famous for his novel 'Robinson Crusoe', wrote in a letter in 1724 that "Rochester, Strood and Chatham were three distinct places but contiguous except the interval of the river between the first two and a very small marsh or vacancy between Rochester and Chatham". Nowadays those three towns, along with Gillingham and Rainham, are even more firmly welded together in the vast conurbation of the Medway Towns, although Strood is clear enough because it's on the other side of the river. A later writer, William Cobbett (1763-1835), noted in 'Rural Rides' (p.42) that "Rochester and Chatham form one main street of about two miles and a half in length".

Rochester, which is about 30 miles from London, is distinct from the other towns because it is the lowest bridging point of the River Medway, although since 1996 there has been a lower public crossing of the river following the construction of a road tunnel between Gillingham and Strood. The Romans built a bridge across the Medway as part of Watling Street, carrying traffic from London to Dover. A wooden bridge existed in Rochester from at least the year 960, and in 1264 Simon de Montfort set fire to it as part of his successful attempt to take control of the town. In the winter of 1380–81 a large proportion of the repaired bridge was washed away. A 14-foot wide stone bridge was then built in its place between 1387 and 1392, paid for by the profits of pillage from the French during the Hundred Years War.

Rochester Bridge was so vital to commerce in the region that in 1449 the Archbishop of Canterbury offered a remission of sins to those who contributed to its repair. In 1856, when modern river traffic demanded a new structure, the medieval bridge was demolished by the Royal Engineers. To replace it, a cast iron bridge was built by the following year, and that in turn was reconstructed and reopened for traffic in 1914. To increase capacity, a second road bridge was opened next to the first one in 1970. In 1963, a viaduct (widened in 2003) was constructed over the Medway south of Rochester to carry the M2 motorway, and in 2003 an adjacent railway bridge was built for High Speed 1.

There were probably prehistoric, and definitely Celtic, settlements in Rochester. The Romans established an important base called 'Durobrivae' where Watling Street crossed the Medway. The Anglo-Saxons called it 'Hrofesceaster', from which the present name derives.

Rochester Cathedral is Britain's second oldest (after Canterbury), having been founded as a priory in 604 by Bishop Justus in the reign of Ethelbert of Kent, the first English king to convert to Christianity. The original structure of the cathedral was Saxon, but the current building is Norman, dating from around 1080 and constructed on the orders of Bishop Gundulf. He was a monk from the abbey of Bec in Normandy who came to England in 1070 as the assistant to the Archbishop of Canterbury, and he was sent to Rochester as bishop in 1077. His talent for architecture had been spotted by William I, and because of his engineering ability, Gundulf is sometimes referred to as 'The father of the Corps of Royal Engineers'. However, much of his work at Rochester Cathedral has been obscured by the masonry of the 12th to 14th century additions. The spire wasn't added until 1904.

For centuries, Rochester was of great strategic importance because of its position near the confluence of the Thames and the Medway. In addition to laying the foundations of Rochester Cathedral, in the reign of William II (1087-1100), Gundulf undertook work on Rochester Castle, which was built to guard the river crossing. It stands on the site of a Roman fort and has Britain's tallest keep (fortified tower). It was the scene of two sieges, in 1215 by King John when the barons were rebelling, and in 1264 by Simon de Montfort. The wife of Robert Bruce, who was king of Scotland from 1306 until 1329, was briefly a prisoner in Rochester Castle in 1314. The castle was badly damaged during the Peasants' Revolt and then gradually fell out of use.

Rochester was the only Medway town until the 16th century, when Henry VIII decided to use Chatham for naval purposes. Although a settlement existed at Chatham in Anglo-Saxon times, and it was mentioned in the Domesday Book as 'Ceteham', the place had previously been a village of little importance. It was then developed by Henry's daughter, Elizabeth I, into a royal naval dockyard, and by the reign of Charles II (1660-1685) it had become England's chief naval station. Chatham was only a day's ride from London and was close to Kentish hardwoods, the gun foundries of the Medway, and the powder makers of the Swale (which is a tidal channel of the Thames Estuary that separates the Isle of Sheppey from the rest of Kent). HMS Victory, which was then the largest warship in the world with 100 guns, was built at Chatham between 1758 and 1765.

Upnor Castle was constructed on the orders of Elizabeth I and is located on the west bank of the Medway, opposite and a short distance downriver from Chatham Dockyard. It was intended to protect both the dockyard and ships anchored in the Medway, but it was largely neglected and its garrison of about 80 men couldn't prevent the humiliation which the unexpected Dutch raid in June 1667 inflicted. That was what brought Samuel Pepys to the Medway Towns. His mission was to strengthen the castle (which he did, sadly, with stone taken from the keep of Rochester Castle), and to bolster the defence of Chatham Dockyard. Upnor Castle was used as a store for ordnance (military supplies, weapons and ammunition) from 1668 until 1827. At one point it stored more gunpowder than the Tower of London.

By the 18th century, Chatham Dockyard was the largest industrial employer in Kent, and in the 19th century it was building ships-of-the-line, steam sailboats, iron-clad hulls and then modern all-metal boats. Over the course of more than 400 years it provided in excess of 500 ships for the Royal Navy. At its height it was employing at least 10,000 skilled workers and covered 400 acres. It expanded rapidly from about 1865 onwards, and by the early 20th century two-thirds of the dockyard was in Gillingham. At a time when the primary purpose of education was seen as training youngsters to be part of a compliant workforce, rather than preparing them for life in general, this growth had an effect on what was taught in local schools; boys attended dockyard classes and sat a dockyard examination.

It seems hard to comprehend that Gillingham was once mostly farmland with a small population, but mainly because of that expansion of the dockyard its population increased from 4,153 in the 1801 census to 42,643 in 1901. Rochester grew from 7,989 in 1801 to 27,619 in 1901, while between the same dates the population of Chatham rose from 10,505 to 36,944. The Medway Towns rapidly industrialised in the second half of the 19th century, becoming especially known for the making of paper and cement and as an engineering centre. Gillingham remains the largest of the towns, while Chatham is the main shopping centre. Rochester is generally accepted to be the most interesting, although not everyone would agree. A nameless resident told 'Kent Live' in 2019 that Rochester is "damp and full of poor people in cheap market clothing who look like they have a week to live". Another remarked that "people like to boast about the Strand Leisure Park in Gillingham, but it's just a bit of grass with a swimming pool that sits by the side of a disgustingly filthy river". Everyone's entitled to their opinions, aren't they?

Gillingham may have its "bit of grass", but it doesn't have the same depth of history as Rochester and Chatham, although it has had a few famous residents. These include Will Adams (1564-1620), a navigator and shipbuilder who joined the navy under the command of Francis Drake and saw service against the Spanish Armada in 1588. Adams became the first Englishman to reach Japan in 1600; James Clavell's novel 'Shogun' is based on his life. A more recent celebrity to grow up in Gillingham was David Frost (1939- 2013), who was a television host, journalist and satirist.

In the 1960s and 1970s it was a common cry of local Conservatives that Medway residents should "vote Tory to save the dockyard", whipping up fears that a Labour government would make defence cuts that included closing it. All too often Tory promises are broken, and it was Thatcher's government which announced the closure of Chatham Dockyard in 1981. However, with the invasion of the Falkland Islands in 1982, redundancy notices were withdrawn and the dockyard was heavily involved in preparing ships for the war and in repairing them on their return. The Tory government then closed the dockyard in 1984 with the loss of 7,000 jobs, causing severe and long-lasting economic hardship to the Medway Towns, especially to Gillingham. There is now a maritime museum on part of the site, where visitors can go aboard three historic warships – a Victorian sloop, a World War II destroyer, and a submarine from the Cold War era.

The Chatham Lines were a number of forts built on a hill to the east of the town from 1756 onwards. They were upgraded in 1803 (for example, the ditch walls were rebuilt in brick) because of the Napoleonic Wars (1793-1815), although they were never used. They were massively re-fortified during World War Two, with the ditch acting as an anti-tank barrier. They are now designated a 'Scheduled Ancient Monument'. About forty years after he had joined the army in 1783, Cobbett (p.42) wrote of Chatham: "Upon looking up towards the fortifications and the barracks, how many recollections crowded into my mind!"

Fort Amherst is the best surviving example in Britain of a Georgian fortress, and it's the largest one from the Napoleonic era. It is located in Chatham, close to the Town Hall and just off Dock Road in the direction of Gillingham. It was built in 1756 to protect Chatham Dockyard from any landward attack. In 1820, a sentry in the fort noticed the outbreak of the Great Fire of Chatham, and as a result soldiers were sent into the town to wake people, which saved many lives.

Chapter 3

Napoleon and Wellington

At the beginning of July 1789, the price of bread in France was 55% higher than it had been two years earlier. On 14 July it reached a new peak. The people of Paris, along with starving peasants from the surrounding countryside, reacted violently and stormed the Bastille, a large prison fortress which was seen as a symbol of royal authority. This event marked the beginning of the French Revolution, and throughout France peasants began to attack their lords, many of whom had treated them little better than slaves.

The leaders of the revolution thought that the main threat to them came from outside France. Hundreds of aristocrats were fleeing to other countries and were urging the monarchs of Europe to help them crush the revolution. Largely in self defence, the revolutionary government declared war on Austria and Prussia in April 1792 and on Britain in February 1793.

By the end of 1793 many people, including Louis XVI and his wife Marie Antoinette, had been guillotined and France had become a republic. In 1790 the Irish parliamentarian Edmund Burke prophesied that in France "bloodshed and disorder will give place to a military tyrant". Sure enough, in 1799 Napoleon Bonaparte (1769-1821) overthrew the revolutionary government and became dictator of France, before going on to crown himself Emperor of France in 1804.

In November 1806, Napoleon issued a decree excluding British ships from ports on the mainland of Europe, and forbidding the importation of British goods into any part of Europe under his control or allied with him. Russia and Prussia both agreed to enforce this decree, and within a few months they, as well as Austria, declared war on Britain. This was part of Napoleon's plan to blockade Britain and paralyse British commerce. This hurt British industries and helped spur the Luddite protest movement against unemployment.

Perhaps the heyday of the Medway Towns was during the Napoleonic Wars. The effects of the blockade bore some similarity to those of the self-inflicted calamity of Brexit. British exports to Northern Europe fell by two-thirds in real terms between 1805 and 1808. Imports of grain from Europe fell from 114,000 tons in 1807 to 14,000 tons in 1808, and the price of wheat increased nearly 60% between 1807 and 1810. When Britain responded with a counter-blockade, Chatham Dockyard became very busy, rapidly producing ships-of-the-line for the war effort.

The war between Britain and France remained in a state of deadlock for several years. Britain's wealth and advanced industries should have enabled her to crush France, but Napoleon was a military genius. Furthermore, the British army was small and badly organised. The pay was poor, discipline was harsh and the lower ranks had to be filled mainly with men from jails and workhouses. Most of the officers were wealthy men with little knowledge of military matters who bought their rank for social reasons. (It had become a pattern in many families of the landed gentry that while the eldest son would inherit the estate and enter politics, the second son would join the army, and the third son would go into the church or become a lawyer.)

In 1808, while the Spanish were rebelling against French rule, a small British expeditionary force commanded by the Duke of Wellington (1769-1852) landed in Portugal. Wellington built a series of fortifications near Lisbon in 1809 called The Torres Vedras Lines. He then wore down the French army in Spain with brief campaigns followed by orderly retreat behind the defences.

On 8 March 1812, the British began the siege of Badajoz. So that the attackers could move up the walls with a degree of safety, someone had to dig trenches for them to walk along. These trenches were called 'saps', and the men who dug them were 'sappers'. Wellington had few sappers, and so the infantry, who were not trained for it and were therefore not very good at it, had to do the work. Nevertheless, Badajoz was captured on 7 April.

On that same day, Wellington wrote a forceful letter to Lord Liverpool, who at that time was secretary of state for war (he became prime minister in June of that year after the assassination of Spencer Perceval). Heavy losses had been sustained in the sieges in Spain, and Wellington strongly recommended the formation of a corps of sappers and miners. The letter had immediate and positive results. A royal warrant was issued on 23 April 1812 by the Prince Regent (on behalf of the insane George III), authorising an establishment for the instruction of sapping, mining and other military fieldworks. Charles Pasley was chosen to be the first director of the new Royal Engineer Establishment. In May 1812, he received orders at Plymouth to march with a detachment of men to Chatham, which was the place selected for setting up the establishment. It was probably favoured to Plymouth because of its proximity to the headquarters of the Royal Military Artificers at Woolwich.

Military engineers, such as Bishop Gundulf, had been brought to England by William I in the 11th century. However, the origins of the modern corps, along with those of the Royal Artillery, lie in the Board of Ordnance which was established in the 15th century with its headquarters in the Tower of London. In May 1716 at Woolwich, the Board established the Corps of Engineers, consisting only of 28 commissioned officers. The manual work was, of course, done by civilian artisans and labourers.

As previously described, Chatham was a strongly fortified naval dockyard town, and its defences were of a permanent nature and designed to be garrisoned by some 7,000 men. The fortifications provided excellent material for instruction in the art of siege warfare, and ample land for fieldwork training was available at Upnor on the western bank of the River Medway. There were also natural and ready-made facilities for wet and dry bridging. Rochester Bridge then had many narrow spans and the Medway was tidal; the water rushing between the piers made navigation hazardous and provided just those risks which Pasley considered suitable for realistic pontoon training.

The first unit trained at Chatham and sent to join Wellington distinguished itself at the storming of San Sebastian in 1813, and its men were nicknamed 'Pasley's Cadets'. Soon after this, Wellington was able to advance right across Spain and over the Pyrenees into France. When the Peninsular War (the conflict that involved Portugal, Spain and Britain against France) ended in the early months of 1814, there were five companies of Royal Engineers serving with Wellington's army.

Wellington arrived at Toulouse in April 1814, where he found out that the French had already surrendered. Napoleon was banished to the island of Elba, but he escaped in March 1815 and rallied enough support to resume the war. From Paris he collected an army and marched towards Brussels, where Wellington and the British were stationed. However, Napoleon was finally defeated at Waterloo, just over nine miles south of Brussels, on 18 June 1815. The victorious coalition included Prussian troops led by Blücher and British, Dutch and Belgian troops under Wellington.

Who deserves the most credit for that victory was discussed at an international conference of history teachers more than sixty years ago. Dance (p.21) says it was Wellington – according to the delegates from Britain, the USA and Italy. Blücher, said the German teachers. The French gave it first to Blücher and secondly to Wellington. The Austrian and Norwegian delegates gave it to Wellington and Blücher equally. The Dutchman at the conference declined to give a reply, while the Belgian said that the battle would have been lost if a Belgian general had not ignored Wellington's signal to retreat! Typically, English historian P.F.Speed (p.96) insists that "in helping to overthrow

Napoleon, Wellington's army had done far more, in proportion to its size, than any other army in Europe". Furthermore, Pasley's Cadets had proved the value of the new Royal Engineer Establishment at Chatham.

Napoleon was again banished, this time to the island of Saint Helena in the South Atlantic, where he died six years later. Lord Liverpool remained prime minister until 1827; Wellington became a member of his cabinet in 1819 and later went on to become prime minister himself for two short periods of time.

Chapter 4

Charles Pasley

Do you remember that annoying kid in your class at school who seemed to be good at every subject? That could have been Charles Pasley. He was born in Dumfriesshire in 1780 and, it is claimed, was able to translate the New Testament from Greek at the age of eight. When he was twelve, he wrote a history of some skirmishes in Scotland and then allegedly translated it into Latin in imitation of the style of the Roman historian Levy.

Pasley entered the Royal Military Academy at Woolwich in 1796. In the following year he obtained a commission in the Royal Artillery, was transferred to the Corps of Engineers in 1798 and was fast-tracked to the position of first lieutenant in 1799. Between 1799 and 1807 he served in Minorca, Malta, Naples and Sicily, and he was employed on various important and sometimes confidential missions; for example, he was sent from Malta to communicate with Lord Nelson in 1804. His meteoric rise through the ranks continued; he was a second captain by 1805 and a first captain by 1807. He was present at the siege of Vlissingen in 1809, where he volunteered to lead a storming party. Pasley was wounded twice, firstly by a bayonet in the thigh and then by a bullet in the spine. The second injury caused him to be invalided for a year, during which time he learned German. He would later be taught the Welsh and Irish languages by sappers from Wales and Ireland.

Between 1810 and 1812, Pasley wrote four essays on military policy, and they were received favourably in high places. He stressed the need for "forming a well-instructed and well-disciplined body of engineer soldiers diligently exercised in all operations of a siege, particularly military mining, and also in the formation of military bridges". With the intention of improving the practice of military engineering, Pasley began a course of instruction for his non-commissioned officers. He was probably the most obvious person to become the first director of the new Royal Engineer Establishment at Chatham in 1812, and with the appointment came yet another promotion, this time to the rank of major. By the end of 1814 he was a lieutenant-colonel.

Pasley wrote three textbooks on military instruction between 1814 and 1817. The first covered practical geometry and contained principles of plan drawing. The second and third were about elementary fortification, including the principles of the science and rules for construction. All three books were published by John Murray. He then wrote a volume on how the army was supplied with provisions, having concluded that his men had been "most grossly ill-treated by the army bread contractor". In 1818 Pasley published a volume entitled 'Standing Orders', consisting of a complete code of rules and duties for all ranks in the army.

Pasley's method of instruction was quite revolutionary for the early 19th century. At that time few soldiers could read or write, and it was considered that to educate them and to teach non-commissioned officers to carry out fieldworks on their own responsibility would be a waste of time. Some of the military hierarchy even thought that it might make them conceited and insubordinate. However, writing in 'The Royal Engineers Journal' (p.3), Lt-Col Sandeman confirmed that other ranks were, because of Pasley's initiative, given instruction in 'the three Rs'. Soldiers were taught the common rules in arithmetic and decimal fractions and even the use of logarithms. They were also encouraged to write neatly and clearly!

Pontooning is the art of constructing a temporary bridge over a river, using a series of boats or floating vessels joined together with road-bearers on which the road decking is placed. Pasley developed a new form of pontoon bridge which was adopted by the army in 1817. Each pontoon was split into two halves, so that two pointed ends could be connected together in instances where there was tidal flow, as in the River Medway. Each half was enclosed, which reduced the risk of swamping, and there were multiple lashing points. Every year the Royal Engineers would construct a pontoon bridge across the Medway in the presence of the local infantry and the cavalry from Maidstone, who would then cross the bridge. 'The Pasley Pontoon' lasted until it was replaced in 1836.

As a member of Lord Liverpool's cabinet in the early 1820s, the Duke of Wellington directed that military architecture should form part of the study of junior officers at the R. E. Establishment. As a result, Pasley started a course on architecture there in 1825.

In February 1825, Pasley carried out the first experiment in firing a charge under water. This was ignited through a fuse, probably made of lead. He was later responsible for the first submarine charge to be fired by electricity; it was exploded in September 1839 against the wreck of a battleship which had been sunk at Spithead. Many other wrecks were dealt with in a similar manner in subsequent years. Diving became a recognised Royal Engineer trade, and the science of submarine mining began to be studied at the Chatham establishment; a diving bell had been invented there by 1836. In 1837, the work of the Royal Engineers was extended to Chatham Dockyard.

Portland cement, so named because of its similarity to a type of building stone quarried on the Isle of Portland in Dorset, was developed from natural cements made in Britain from around 1750. In 1824, Joseph Aspdin in Wakefield patented Portland cement, and his son William improved it. In 1826, Charles Pasley began research and experiments on artificial cement, and in 1830 he made a chance discovery of the hydraulic properties of cement manufactured from chalk and Medway clay. That had a lasting local effect. The first cement works in Rochester was opened in 1851; in 1896, 5,311 tons of cement were exported from Rochester, which had a value of £7,549. At the turn of the century, the greater part of the Portland cement made in England was manufactured on the banks of the Thames (near Dartford and Gravesend) and the Medway. Writing in 1909, Colonel Ward of the Royal Engineers (p.18) concluded that "from a constructional point of view, the invention of Portland cement ranks probably, with Bessemer's improvements in steel manufacture and the use of reinforced concrete, as one of the three most important inventions in the 19th century".

Pasley wrote a textbook on the practical operations of a siege, in which every stage was treated as a separate study. It was translated into French and published in Paris. Siege operations were first organised by Pasley on Chatham Lines in 1833, in which all the arms of the garrison took part. When a mine was exploded on 18 June that year, it was of some significance, since field manoeuvres were not instituted generally until after the Crimean War (1853-6). However, siege operations were again carried out at the RE Establishment in 1844, 1846 and 1848 when Sir Frederick Smith was the director.

Pasley was director of the RE Establishment at Chatham from 1812 until 1841. 'The Dictionary of National Biography', Vol 43 (p.441), suggests that during that time "there was hardly any subject in connection with his profession as a military man and an engineer that did not benefit by his attention". He was Europe's leading demolitions expert and siege warfare specialist. When Pasley left the establishment to become inspector general of railways, he was again promoted, this time to major-general. He retired in 1846 and died in London in 1861, but not before he had been made a general.

Charles Pasley's eldest son (also named Charles) was born in Chatham in 1824 and educated at the King's School Rochester. He was commissioned in the Royal Engineers in 1843 and served on the staff of the Great Exhibition in 1851. Pasley Junior became superintendent of Chatham Dockyard in 1865, overseeing a major extension during the following eight years. He died in 1890.

Chapter 5

Steam Engines and Railways

Railways resulted from a combination of two ideas. These were the mounting of a steam engine on a carriage so as to use its power to propel that and other attached carriages, and the propulsion of such carriages along tracks made of parallel lines. In 1802, a Cornish engineer called Richard Trevithick (1771-1833) patented a high-pressure steam engine, and in 1804 it made a journey along ten miles of tramway in South Wales. In 1808, Trevithick displayed this locomotive on a circular track in London. The idea aroused interest in coal-mining areas, and a colliery fireman in Northumberland named George Stephenson (1781- 1848) developed a better locomotive. Edward Pease, a wealthy landowner, employed Stephenson to survey and construct a public railway on a 27-mile route connecting coal mines in South Durham to the river port of Stockton, and as a result the Stockton to Darlington line was opened in September 1825. The Liverpool to Manchester line followed in 1830, and the great age of the railways had begun.

In the early days there was much opposition to the railways, as there often is to anything new. Vested interests, such as those who had put their capital into coaches and road travel or canals, not to mention 'nimby' country gentlemen who wished to preserve the peace and quiet of their estates, did what they could to hinder railway development. Nevertheless, by 1840 there were already 1,857 miles of railway track in Britain, and by 1843 London was linked with Brighton, Southampton, Bristol, Birmingham, Leicester and York.

There was no attempt to plan a proper railway network and Parliament allowed a 'free for all' which, for example, saw two companies – the London, Chatham and Dover (originally known as the East Kent Railway) and the South Eastern – vie for supremacy on the same route. However, Charles Pasley was made inspector general of railways in 1841, and he checked many new lines, criticising the speed with which some were opened with poor engineering standards. Ironically, Pasley himself faced criticism in 1846 for approving a line between Edinburgh and Berwick on which the bridges and earthworks failed to withstand heavy rain, and where 19 miles of track were rendered unusable. Pasley approved the temporary works which were undertaken to restore a service, but even some of the new work proved faulty. For once in his life, Pasley's halo had slipped. The railway inspectorate was reorganised soon afterwards with no position for him in the new structure. He retired, but was still given a knighthood.

The main railway lines in Britain were constructed between 1833 and 1862, and most of them were planned by George Stephenson or his son Robert. The mileage of track in Britain increased from 6,600 in 1850 to 8,900 in 1854 and to 13,600 by 1870.

The earliest of the Dover to London main lines, built by the South Eastern Railway, was completed by 1844. The route ran from Dover to Folkestone and Ashford, and then virtually straight for 46 miles through the Vale of Kent to Redhill via Tonbridge. At this time, the railway provision in north Kent was very poor, even though both Rochester and Chatham had become sizeable towns. In 1846, the South Eastern Railway purchased the Thames and Medway Canal Tunnel near Higham and laid railway tracks through it, and by 1847 trains went from Strood to Gravesend. By 1849 there was a through train service between London and Rochester, although the terminus station was at the canal basin in Strood with a ferry provided to Rochester. A large meeting was held at Rochester in January 1850 to discuss the need for a railway connecting Strood to Dover, but although the idea of an independent railway was adopted, the plans came to nothing.

A railway from Faversham to Chatham did open in 1858, and it was extended to Strood across the new Medway Bridge which had been completed in the previous year. It was a single track line, only 18.5 miles in length, and it had taken five years to construct. The service was only five trains a day in each direction, and the journey time was 50 minutes. Regular through services were possible between London Victoria and Canterbury East by the end of 1860. At that time, there were no stops in either Bromley or Gillingham (the latter was called New Brompton in those days and was still only a minor suburb of Chatham). The development of these railways made the River Medway far less important for the import and export of goods.

In 1899, those rival companies, the London, Chatham and Dover and the South Eastern, agreed to share operations, work them as a single system and pool the receipts, but they remained separate companies. During World War I, the government took control of all railways. Afterwards, through the Railways Act of 1921, the government decided on a compulsory amalgamation of the railways into four large groups. As a result, the London, Chatham and Dover and the South Eastern companies became part of Southern Railway in January 1923.

The steam engine was first introduced into the curriculum of the Royal Engineers in 1870. The first railway ever used for military purposes had been laid in 1856 from Balaclava to the plateau on which the siege works were constructed during the Crimean War. This line was laid by a civilian contractor, but later the construction of trench tramways was introduced as part of the regular work of Royal Engineers in siege operations.

In 1870-1, a trench tramway was constructed from Black Lion Field in New Brompton to the wall of Chatham Dockyard. This railway was used for the conveyance of fieldwork stores from the army workshops to the various batteries and other siege works which were increasingly being constructed in the neighbourhood. A line was also laid at Upnor to take steam sapper locomotives which ran on flanged wheels. This was the origin of the training of sappers in locomotive work. The 'steam sapper' was first used operationally in the Second Ashanti War of 1873-4 (some sources call it the third!), in which the Ashanti (of what is now Ghana) were defeated and their capital Kumasi, destroyed.

A gunpowder magazine had been constructed at Upnor between 1856 and 1857, and Chattenden Barracks was built on the Hoo Peninsula between 1872 and 1873 to accommodate a fieldworks party. The Upnor railway was used for the conveyance of building materials to Chattenden, where five magazines were built on a hillside by the Royal Engineers in 1875. The line later served the site of a fort at Hoo, but it seems doubtful whether this line continued in use after its primary purpose had been served. However, the course of the line was found convenient in 1885 for an experimental railway built by the Royal Engineers, and this was used for training. It was constructed on a narrow gauge that has never been used extensively in Britain, but it was adopted for numerous strategic and secondary lines in India. In 1906, the Chattenden and Upnor Railway passed into the hands of the Admiralty, and soon afterwards it was used as an inter-works line.

Chapter 6

The Royal Engineers after Pasley

Pasley was succeeded as director of the RE Establishment first by Sir Frederick Smith and then by Lt-Col Harry Jones. The Board of Ordnance was abolished in 1855, and in 1856, at the end of the Crimean War, the Royal Engineers were amalgamated with the Royal Sappers and Miners to become a unified Corps of Royal Engineers based at Chatham. (The barracks of the Royal Engineers are generally referred to as being in Chatham, but they are actually at Brompton in Gillingham.) In 1869, the name of the Royal Engineer Establishment was changed to the School of Military Engineering (SME), and the title of director was changed to commandant. It was men from this school who designed the Victoria and Albert Museum (which was paid for with some of the profits from the Great Exhibition of 1851) and the Albert Hall, which opened in 1871.

The Crimean War was a success in that it prevented Russia from getting naval access to the Mediterranean Sea, but it resulted in the death of 25,000 British troops, along with about 100,000 French soldiers and up to a million Russians, almost all of cholera, dysentery and neglect. The war also highlighted the gross inefficiency and advancing years of the British commanders, most of whom, as usual, aristocrats. The

British commander-in-chief was Lord Raglan, who was 66 when he reached the Crimea and who had been a close friend of the Duke of Wellington. Raglan had last fought at Waterloo in 1815 and still frequently referred to the enemy as "the French", even though they were on the British side in this war. Had he not died in the year before the war started, it's not completely beyond the realms of possibility that Wellington himself (who would by then have been 84) could have been summoned up to command the forces; he had, after all, organised a military force in 1848 to protect London from the 'danger' of Chartists wanting an extension of democracy.

Hansard (11 July 1856) reported how Leicester Vernon, the MP for Chatham, complained in Parliament that at the siege of Sebastopol "there were only 300 or 400 sappers where there should have been as many thousands – for behind the earthworks was ranged the whole military power of Russia – and where, if there had been as many thousands, it would have saved thousands of lives and millions of money." Vernon continued: "There were 80 officers of engineers sent to the Crimea; of these 43 were killed, wounded or put hors de combat (rendered incapable of performing their duties) – a wholesale slaughter without a parallel." Nevertheless, while others were highlighting the extreme inefficiency of the military supply system and most of the commanders, Vernon was praising the Royal Engineers for playing a significant part in the turning points of the war.

Army reforms, which begun half-heartedly after the Crimean War, were renewed when British governments became alarmed by Prussia's rapid victories over Denmark in 1864, Austria in

1866 and France in 1870-1. The Prussian system of professional soldiers with up-to-date weapons was far superior to the traditional system of gentleman soldiers that Britain used. Edward Cardwell, who was war secretary from 1868 to 1874 in William Gladstone's first Liberal government, abolished the purchase of commissions in the army, despite predictably fierce opposition from the Tories. The middle class ideal of selection by merit and education had been found previously only in the artillery and engineers. Lord Cardigan, who led the disastrous Charge of the Light Brigade in the Crimea, had paid the equivalent of £2 million in today's money to purchase his commission. Cardwell also created reserve forces stationed in Britain by establishing short terms of service for enlisted men (six years of service followed by six years in the reserve).

Desertion by soldiers was dealt with harshly as a deterrent to others; writing in 1895, R.G.Hobbes (p.103) tells us that "the punishment would at all events be sore and disgraceful". A deserter could expect a short term of imprisonment, to be branded with a 'D' on some part of his anatomy, and probably a flogging. Before 1838, the punishment may have been 400 or 500 lashes, which in most cases would have been tantamount to a death sentence. In 1838, corporal punishment was limited to 200 lashes, and in 1848 it had been further reduced to 50 lashes. In 1868, Cardwell abolished flogging in peacetime; it was ended on active service in 1880.

The Royal Engineers provided the second largest source of civilian employment in the Medway Towns in the 19th century, but numerically they always fell a long way short of Chatham Dockyard. Many of the civilians they employed were ex-army; a large number of Royal Engineers finished their service at Chatham and then settled locally. The number of recruits taken in by the Royal Engineers was about 450 a year, some of whom would be from the Medway Towns. 'The Chatham News' (14 January 1871) reported how notices would be issued at Chatham promoting "the advantages to be gained by men who enter this distinguished branch of the service". The recruits had to be tradesmen, clerks, surveyors or draughtsmen, and 33 trades were listed on these notices, stating what kind of men were wanted.

Many men were not enlisted locally, and until 1870 recruits from other parts of the country would be escorted to Chatham by a recruiting sergeant. Hobbes (p.101) says "these men looked as if they had been cut from their moorings and had drifted down the stream of life until taken in tow by the rubicund soldier who led them into this kindly port". Occasionally the men who were enlisted were not what the locals wanted. Cases in the Medway courts of stealing were not infrequent, and sometimes there would be general public indignation. 'The Chatham News' (13 October 1860) describes how strong remonstrances would be presented to the military authorities "on the subject of these reiterated crimes by soldiers, urging that the army be not recruited with an utter disregard of the character of the men admitted as soldiers".

'The Chatham News' (12 May 1860) also reported on its front page how "a very valuable invention" by Sergeant Sturrock of the Royal Engineers improved revolving and repeating firearms. His new rifle or pistol was double-barrelled , and there were two series of chambers (or one for each barrel) in the cylinder.

Either of the series of chambers was discharged in the ordinary manner; then, by a change of the hammer, the other series could be fired. The invention required only a slight modification to be applicable to any revolver.

As a result of the experience gained in the Crimean campaign, the study of telegraphy, photography and scientific subjects generally was carried out at the SME under a special instructor, and in 1871 a laboratory was set up for the course in photography. In the late 1860s, Chatham was home to the leading military scientific school in Europe.

By 1871, submarine mining had become a subject of sufficient importance at the SME for an assistant director to be specifically allotted to it. Submarine mining had been brought to the notice of the world during the American Civil War (1861-5), and after 1863 a series of experiments had been conducted at Chatham in order to determine the best system of mine defence. In 1866, the 'Floating Experimental School' had been established in the River Medway on an Admiralty lighter (a flat-bottomed barge used to transfer goods and passengers to and from moored ships). However, by 1892 the requirements of the submarine mining service had outgrown the capacity of the Chatham school, and new schools were opened at Portsmouth and Plymouth. In 1905, submarine mining became a responsibility of the Royal Navy.

The first siege manoeuvres after the amalgamation of the Royal Engineers with the Royal Sappers and Miners took place in 1868, and they consisted entirely of mining operations. Some more manoeuvres were carried out in 1871 after repeated postponements, and then again in 1873 and 1877. No further siege manoeuvres took place at Chatham in the next thirty years, possibly because the experience of the Franco- Prussian War of 1870-1 had encouraged the view that fortresses could be taken by blockade.

The Royal Engineers began to explore the possibilities of using air balloons for aerial observation purposes, and their first balloon factory was established at Chatham in 1882. Experiments had been carried out at Woolwich Arsenal as early as 1872 in order to determine the best apparatus for the production of hydrogen gas, and in 1882 further experiments were carried out at Chatham. In 1884, a balloon detachment accompanied an expedition to Bechuanaland in Southern Africa, and another detachment was sent out to the Sudan early in 1885. Both returned to Chatham in the summer of 1885, and some land was purchased at Lidsing (about five miles from Chatham) where summer camps for the balloon detachments were held for the next three years. A balloon school was set up by the Royal Engineers at Brompton in 1888, but in 1891 both the balloon factory and school were moved from Chatham to Aldershot.

This interest in aeronautics developed into an enthusiasm for fixed winged aircraft, and military flying began at Eastchurch on the Isle of Sheppey. Until the Royal Flying Corps was founded in 1912, flying was the province of the Royal Engineers. In 1918, the Royal Flying Corps was amalgamated with the Royal Naval Air Service to form the Royal Air Force.

Chapter 7

Sappers and 20th Century Conflicts

Hot air balloons were used for observation and directing artillery during the Boer War of 1899-1902. This was a bitter colonial conflict between the British and the descendants of Dutch settlers in South Africa. Following some initial setbacks and a long period of guerrilla warfare, the British eventually prevailed, but only after adopting some controversial tactics. These included a 'scorched earth' policy, getting the Royal Engineers to blow up Boer farms, destroying crops and livestock and about 30,000 homesteads. This left thousands of Boer women and children homeless, so the British army kept them in concentration camps in appalling conditions. As well as being a barbaric policy, it was tactically stupid; by relieving the Boers of responsibility for their families, they could concentrate on fighting.

During the Boer War, the Royal Engineers designed and developed a system of blockhouses (small fortifications which allowed their defenders to fire in various directions) and barbed-wire barriers, both of which helped to localise and isolate the Boers' forces and bring the conflict to an end. The Engineers took from the enemy, repaired and ran about 1,400 miles of railway and the telegraph system of both the Orange Free State and the Transvaal. In a despatch in April 1901, Lord Frederick

Roberts, who led the British forces for a year, reported "that there were 27 bridges and 41 culverts (structures that allow water to flow under a road or railway) repaired". He added that "this work was done either by Royal Engineers or by soldiers or native labour acting under Royal Engineer officers".

The Boer War showed that the British army was in desperate need of reform, and the man who set about that task was Richard Haldane, the war secretary in the Liberal government which took office in 1906. Haldane had studied at a German university and realised that the British army was inefficient when compared with the German one. He set up a general staff and reorganised the army - without any addition to its numbers and with an actual reduction in cost. He established an expeditionary force of six divisions, which were ready for immediate service abroad. A territorial army of semi-trained troops was created, and the volunteer corps from universities and public schools provided the officers. Haldane left the war office in 1912, and when World War I began in 1914 the tabloid press falsely claimed that he was pro-German and drove him out of political life. However, he later joined Labour and served in the party's first government in 1924.

On 1 August 1914, the Royal Engineers consisted of 1,056 officers and 10,394 men of the regular army and the reserve, plus 513 officers and 13,127 men serving in the territorial force. Three years later, it had grown to a total manpower of 295,668, and by 1918 to around 315,000. This was because World War I was dependent on engineering. Without the Royal Engineers, there would have been no supplies to the armies, because they maintained the railways, roads, water supply, bridges and transport. They also operated the railways and inland waterways. Without them, there would have been no communications, because they maintained the telephones, wireless and other signalling equipment. Their duties expanded into digging tunnels under enemy lines, trench building, forestry, quarrying, aerial survey, topographical photography, camouflaging techniques and developing responses to chemical warfare. They designed and built the frontline fortifications, creating cover for the infantry and positions for the artillery.

Manned by many experienced coal miners, the Royal Engineers operated their tunnelling companies with much success until the trench warfare stalemate, which lasted three and a half years, ended. (During that time the trench lines, which had extended from the English Channel to the Swiss border, never varied by more than 20 miles.) Then the Engineers built deep dugouts to protect troops from heavy shelling. Some members of the working class had been able to demonstrate their true value, instead of just being cannon fodder.

The same cannot be said of the graduates of public schools who provided the officers for the army. Cardwell may have abolished the purchase of commissions in 1870, but that didn't prevent incompetent leaders being put in charge. In his 1988 book 'Eton Renewed', former Eton teacher Tim Card wrote (p.301) how "World War I was a public schoolboys' war and was fought to preserve an imperial system which had been good for public schools but not the working classes". Former Harrow pupil John French was head of the army at the start of World War I. Together with the infamous Douglas Haig, the leader of the British Expeditionary Force (BEF) from 1915 (who was nicknamed 'The butcher of the Somme'), he sent many men to slaughter. French was obsessed with cavalry charges against guns, while Haig couldn't grasp the importance of the machine gun. Sadly, in the 21st century we don't seem to have moved on very far, when all it needs is a wealthy family, an Eton education and the right connections for an amoral and incompetent serial liar to become prime minister.

Another former Harrow pupil, Winston Churchill (1874-1965), was the cabinet minister responsible for the disastrous Gallipoli campaign of 1915-16, which resulted in 51,000 deaths on the British side and over 56,600 Turkish deaths. In World War II (1939-45), Churchill, now the prime minister, was also culpable for another fiasco when Dieppe was attacked in August 1942. The aim of the venture was to see if a port under German control could be captured and held for a short period. Within ten hours of the attack, 3,623 men had been killed, wounded or taken prisoner.

Before World War II, recruits for the Royal Engineers had to be at least 5 feet 4 inches tall (5 feet 2 inches for the mounted branch). As Cardwell had prescribed, men would enlist for six years with a further six years with the reserve. Unlike most corps and regiments, in which the upper age limit was 25, men could enlist in the Royal Engineers up to 30 years of age. As they had done since 1812, they continued to train at Chatham, but the mounted depot was at Aldershot.

World War II began when Hitler invaded Poland and ended with that country falling under Russian influence. In 'Posh Boys', Robert Verkaik (p.72) tells us how "the type of privately educated senior officer who had led the BEF in France in 1914 was easily recognisable among the next generation of commanders who were once again drawing up plans to defeat the Germans across the Channel. So we should not be surprised that the war got off to exactly the same disastrous start as the previous one, with a series of morale-sapping defeats."

During World War II, the Royal Engineers did much the same work as in World War 1. They maintained the railways, roads, bridges and water supply, but new roles were added. They became responsible for bomb disposal, mine clearance, airfield construction and the use of tanks adapted for battlefield engineering. The Royal Engineers laid bailey bridges, which were developed in 1940-1 and which were portable and pre-fabricated; they required no special tools or heavy equipment to assemble. Engineers also helped to build and operate the Mulberry harbour which was used for the D-Day landings in Normandy in 1944.

After 1945, the Royal Engineers provided most of the army's contribution to Britain's atomic weapons development programme. Sappers were also involved in the Suez debacle in 1956 and in the Northern Ireland conflict after 1969, where they played an important part in bomb disposal. In the 21st century, the Royal Engineers have served in both Afghanistan and Iraq.

There is a memorial at La Ferté-sous-Jouarre on the River Marne to mark the contribution which the Royal Engineers made in World War I. There is also a memorial to the Royal Engineers at Arromanches in Normandy, which was the site of the

Mulberry harbour. Rochester Cathedral contains more than 25 memorials to individual officers and soldiers of the Corps of Royal Engineers, including stained glass, mosaics and plaques.

When the Royal Sappers and Miners were incorporated into the Corps of Royal Engineers in 1856, the museum at Woolwich was transferred to Chatham and amalgamated with a model room of engineer equipment that had been started at the RE Establishment in 1812. Since 1987, the Royal Engineers Museum in Gillingham has been welcoming visitors. It tells the story of the life, work and sheer inventive genius of soldier engineers from the Romans to the two world wars, and in particular the achievements of the Corps of Royal Engineers. It is a museum and library which holds over 500,000 objects, including the map used by the Duke of Wellington during the Battle of Waterloo and the last surviving Brennan torpedo.

In the early 1980s, an engraved display of some distinguished sappers was made in Sappers Walk, off Gillingham High Street, featuring Charles Gordon, Herbert Kitchener and James McCudden. It also shows some of the inventions of Louis Brennan, who worked closely with the Royal Engineers. Three of those men were killed in accidents and one was murdered.

Chapter 8

Charles Gordon

The man who was murdered was Charles George Gordon. Winston Churchill would later describe him as "so erratic, capricious, utterly unreliable, his mood changed so often, his temper was abominable, he was frequently drunk, and yet with all that he had a tremendous sense of humour and great abilities". Some people might think that Churchill could have been describing himself there (although his 'abilities' have often been exaggerated).

Gordon was born in Woolwich in 1833, the son of a senior artillery officer. He was educated at a minor private school in Taunton and then at a military academy in Woolwich, where religious teaching and physical instruction were as strict as at any of England's public schools. In 1843 he was devastated when his favourite sibling, his sister Emily, died of tuberculosis. After her death, her place as Gordon's favourite sibling was taken by his very religious older sister Augusta, who nudged her brother towards religion.

As a teenager and an army cadet, Gordon was known for a combative streak and tendency to disregard authority and the rules if he thought they were stupid or unjust. This behaviour delayed his graduation by two years, but as a cadet he showed exceptional talents at map-making and in designing fortifications. He was commissioned as a second lieutenant in the Royal Engineers in 1852 and completed his training at Chatham, after which he was promoted to full lieutenant in 1854. He distinguished himself by his reckless bravery in the siege trenches in the Crimean War, where he was wounded by a Russian sniper. In 1859 he was promoted to captain and made assistant instructor in fieldworks at the RE Establishment in Chatham.

In 1862, Gordon's corps of engineers was assigned to strengthen the European trading centre of Shanghai, which was under threat from Taiping rebels who were trying to depose the Chinese emperor. Gordon became the commander of a peasant force of over 3,000 men raised by the Chinese government to defend the city. They defeated the rebels, and for that achievement Gordon was made a mandarin (a senior civil servant responsible only to the emperor). He returned to Kent in 1865, where he became the commanding officer of the Royal Engineers at Gravesend, superintending the construction of forts at the mouth of the River Thames to guard against a possible French invasion. He disapproved of the work he had been assigned to oversee, believing that the forts were just expensive and useless.

While at Gravesend, Gordon spent much of his leisure time developing his own unorthodox brand of Christianity and doing charitable work for the poor. Verkaik (p.36) writes of how "muscular Christianity" was "the defining virtue wholly embraced by the British army and the legions of missionaries who sallied forth across the empire". He adds that "winning wars, crushing cultures and converting pagans was the best way a man could flex his Christian muscles". According to Verkaik, "Gordon was the Victorian figure who best represents the ideal of muscular Christianity".

Following the death of his father, Gordon undertook extensive social work in Gravesend. Before 1870, there was no universal education in Britain, but there was a network of privately funded 'Ragged Schools' which gave free education to some poor children. Gordon taught in such a school for a while, and even took in some of the children to live with him in his own home. He also tried to ensure that homeless boys he found begging on the streets did not go hungry, and he endeavoured to find them homes and jobs.

Following ten years of construction, the Suez Canal was opened in November 1869. Gordon warned against over-reliance on it, arguing that the Russians could easily sink one ship and block the entire canal. As the world found out in March 2021, one large container ship being buffeted by strong winds was enough to put the canal out of use for six days; a sunken ship would have taken much longer to move. Gordon advised the British government that it should consider improving the Cape route to India with a series of bases in Africa and the Indian Ocean.

In 1873, with British government approval, Gordon was appointed governor of the province of Equatoria in the Sudan by the Khedive of Egypt. Between 1874 and 1876, he mapped the upper section of the River Nile and established a line of stations along the river as far south as present day Uganda. He was then promoted to governor general, where he asserted his authority by crushing rebellions and, because of his religious principles, suppressing the slave trade, often diverting military resources to help free slaves. However, exhaustion forced him to resign and return to England in 1880.

Gordon was often bored and would frequently ask the government for an assignment to somewhere dangerous. In 1884, he was granted his wish when he was re-appointed governor general and sent to the Sudan to evacuate civilians from Khartoum. However, this proved impossible because supplies could not reach Khartoum and a relief force was sent too late. In January 1885 the city fell to the Mahdists, followers of a religious fanatic named Muhammad Ahmad al-Mahdi. Gordon was speared to death and the garrison was slaughtered; the first of 10,000 rescuers arrived two days later. Gladstone, the prime minister, was blamed for this. His supporters had been calling him 'the Grand Old Man' (or GOM for short); in the music halls this was reversed to MOG, 'Murderer of Gordon'. However, in his 1918 book 'Eminent Victorians', Lytton Strachey speculated that Gordon need not have allowed himself to get surrounded and caught in Khartoum, suggesting that he defied orders and refused to evacuate the town while it was still possible.

So what sort of man was Gordon? We've read what Churchill thought of him, but were his comments fair? Gordon was honest and paid his men on time and in full. He regularly gave away 90% of his own annual salary, having a strong concern about the poverty he had witnessed, both in the UK and on his military adventures. He was arrogant enough to believe that he always knew what was best, frequently disobeying orders, even from the prime minister. He was difficult to get on with, yet as an officer he showed strong charisma and leadership; he could inspire men to follow him anywhere. On the other hand, as a private individual he had only a few friends and found dealing with strangers difficult. As a soldier he was brave to the point of recklessness, and by the end of his life he apparently had a strong death wish. He was a keen amateur photographer and a chain smoker of Turkish cigarettes.

Gordon's charitable work for the boys (not the girls) of Gravesend has led to accusations that he was a paedophile. Strachey was the first to strongly imply that Gordon may have preyed on the boys he befriended in the Ragged School. The American historian Byron Farwell, in his 1985 book 'Eminent Victorian Soldiers', wrote of Gordon's "unwholesome" interests in the boys he took to live with him. Gordon never married and claimed to have been a celibate. The British journalist and broadcaster Mark Urban says "it is possible that he had sexual feelings for these urchins, but there is no evidence that he ever acted upon them". Urban continues: "We can only speculate that his increasing religious devotion may have been an outward manifestation of an internal struggle against sexual temptation. The best evidence suggests Gordon was a latent homosexual whose sexual repression led him to funnelling his aggression into a military career with a special energy."

In May 1900, a bronze statue of General Gordon on a camel was unveiled in his memory in Brompton Barracks in Gillingham, opposite a memorial to the general who followed him in the Sudan, Herbert Kitchener. In the 1966 film 'Khartoum', Charlton Heston played the part of Gordon and Laurence Olivier played Muhammad Ahmad al-Mahdi.

Chapter 9

Herbert Kitchener

Edward Colston (1636-1721) was a slave trader, and a statue of him in his home town of Bristol was toppled from its plinth and pushed into the docks by protesters in June 2020. Soon afterwards, a nurse from the Medway Hospital started a campaign to have the statue of Herbert Horatio Kitchener on horseback removed from Dock Road in Chatham, where it was erected in 1959. It had been in Khartoum since 1920, but it was no longer welcome there when Sudan became independent in 1956. So why is Kitchener so contentious?

When Lord Roberts was commanding the British forces in the Boer War, he earned himself the dubious distinction of being the inventor of the concentration camp. After Kitchener took over from Roberts in November 1900, he expanded the use of both the 'scorched earth' policy and concentration camps, the conditions in which deteriorated rapidly. They lacked space, food, sanitation, medicine and medical care, leading to rampant disease and a very high death rate. As a result of Kitchener's callous neglect, 26,370 Boer women and children (of whom 81% were children) and around 20,000 black Africans died in those camps. He is remembered in South Africa as the man who let all those people die, and it helps to explain why that Medway nurse describes Kitchener's statue as "an icon of a racist figure".

Apart from all the deaths in the concentration camps, about 6,000 Boers died fighting, and 24,000 Boer prisoners were sent overseas. The British suffered approximately 22,000 deaths in the war, of whom over 14,000 died of disease. The war cost the British government £210 million.

Henry Kitchener (1805-1894) was an officer who left the army early and, after selling his commission, bought some land in Ireland. This was the time of the great famine there (1845-1852), during which about a million people died. It was caused by a potato blight and by the failure of the Tory government in London to ban the export of grain from Ireland. It also refused to repeal an 1829 law which had made the import of foreign corn into the UK (of which the whole of Ireland was then a part) expensive. In 1846, three-quarters of the potato harvest was lost to blight, The Tory government fell in June of that year, but the Whig government which followed was no better, believing that the free market would somehow provide the food that was desperately needed. Between 1845 and 1855, 2.1 million people emigrated from Ireland, with many of them going to the USA.

By the time that Henry Kitchener acquired his land in Ballylongford in County Kerry, most of the starving tenants had died or been evicted already; others were soon kicked out by him. He wasn't a very nice man and he was hardly a great role model for his son, Herbert, who was born in 1850. According to the writer and broadcaster Jeremy Paxman, Henry disliked blankets and preferred his family to sleep under sheets of newspaper sewn together. Paxman added that Henry once punished the young Herbert by staking him out on the lawn with his wrists and ankles tied to croquet hoops.

Mrs Kitchener suffered from tuberculosis, and so the family moved to Switzerland in 1864, but she died soon afterwards. Herbert was educated at a boarding school in Montreux, before returning to England to study at the Royal Military Academy in Woolwich. He was not a particularly talented student, but he was commissioned into the Royal Engineers in January 1871 and spent the next two years at the SME in Brompton.

From 1874, Herbert Kitchener served in Palestine, Egypt and Cyprus as a surveyor. He learned Arabic and prepared detailed topographical maps (showing the forms and features of land surfaces) of the areas. In 1885, he was prominent in the unsuccessful attempt to save General Gordon, and by 1892 he was the commander-in-chief of the Egyptian army. In 1898, he led an Anglo-Egyptian force up the River Nile to re- conquer the Sudan, building a railway as they went and carrying it across the desert to short-circuit the great loop in the river below Khartoum.

Kitchener crushed an army of 52,000 poorly armed desert tribesmen dervishes in 1898 at Omdurman, on the opposite side of the Nile to Khartoum. This battle was also famous for the charge of the 21st Lancers in which Winston Churchill took part. At least 10,000 dervishes were killed, but only 48 British soldiers lost their lives. Churchill was shocked to see the 17,000 wounded dervishes left to their fate on the battlefield, while British ambulances confined their work to the smaller number of British casualties. However, John Pollock, who wrote a two-volume biography of Kitchener between 1998 and 2001, and which was generally sympathetic towards him, claimed that an Egyptian army doctor was appointed to care for the wounded dervishes and treated about 400 of the worst cases.

After the battle, Khartoum was restored as the capital city of the Sudan, and from then until 1956 the country was jointly governed by Britain and Egypt. However, Kitchener's behaviour at Omdurman has been criticised on two counts. Firstly, Churchill wrote to his mother that the victory "had been disgraced by the inhuman slaughter of the wounded, and Kitchener is responsible for this". There is no evidence that Kitchener ordered his men to shoot them, but he did remind his troops before the battle that the enemy were all "murderers of Gordon". Secondly, and which is certainly true, Kitchener blew up the tomb of Muhammad Ahmad al-Mahdi, who had died from typhus a few months after his followers had murdered Gordon and captured Khartoum in 1885.

Kitchener had the Mahdi's bones thrown into the Nile and, according to Churchill, "carried off his head in a kerosene can as a trophy", perhaps to use as an inkpot. This shocked Queen Victoria, who had previously been one of Kitchener's most ardent fans, and it confirmed the view of the Sudanese nationalists that their new rulers were barbarians. So can you blame a member of one of the caring professions for not wanting to drive past a statue of this man every day on her way to work? No doubt some people will argue that it's difficult to judge past decisions by current standards and values, especially as imperialism has been unfashionable for many years, while others will concur that brutality and murder are evil whenever and wherever they have occurred.

Soon after occupying Khartoum in 1898, Kitchener marched 600 miles further up the Nile to Fashoda, where the French had hoisted their flag. On that occasion, Kitchener handled the incident with great diplomacy and a compromise was reached, averting the danger of war between Britain and France.

Maybe it's just a coincidence that after becoming a freemason in 1883, rapid promotions followed for Kitchener. He was made a captain in that year, a lieutenant-colonel in 1885 and a brigadier in 1892. By 1896 he was a major-general, and he became a baron in 1898. By the end of the Boer War he was a viscount. He then became commander-in-chief in India until 1909, where he decided that his task was to reorganise the army to accumulate all authority under himself. Pollock wrote that Kitchener's approach to any obstacle in his path, whether military, social or political, was "to outmanoeuvre the enemy or leave the field". However, when the Indian army was put to the test in Mesopotamia in 1915, it failed because of the inefficiency of his system.

When World War I began in August 1914, Kitchener, now a field marshal, was appointed war secretary. He was one of the few bigwigs to grasp the fact that the war wouldn't be over in six weeks. He at once issued his famous appeal for 100,000 volunteers, and by November a million men had joined the forces. Kitchener was initially very popular, but when it became clear that British weapons were both insufficient and inefficient, he was widely criticised. He believed that the day-to-day plans for an industrialised nation's war machine could be kept in his head. In May 1915, Asquith, the prime minister, created a new ministry of munitions and put Lloyd George in charge of it.

Kitchener was drowned at sea in 1916. He was one of over 700 people killed when the ship in which he was travelling for secret talks with Britain's Russian allies struck a German mine near the Orkney Islands. C.P.Scott, the editor of 'The Manchester Guardian', remarked that "Kitchener could not have done better than to have gone down, as he was a great impediment lately". Needless to say, his 'convenient' death gave rise to a number of conspiracy theories.

Kitchener is most recognisable from the 1914 poster, of which 54 million copies were issued, where he is pictured with the caption: "Britons: Lord Kitchener wants you. Join your country's army! God save the king!" Eight million personal letters were sent, 12,000 mobilisation meetings were held, and 20,000 speeches were delivered by military spokesmen. Sadly, 306 of those who did volunteer to join the British army (or were conscripted from 2016) ended up being shot for desertion. Most were suffering from shell shock, what we would now categorise as post-traumatic stress disorder.

The characteristic traits of Kitchener were that he was brutal, ferociously unforgiving in battle, domineering and autocratic, and that he didn't like teamwork or delegating responsibility. His colleagues viewed his utter failure to manage the power he had accrued to himself with deepening horror. Writing in 1928, Arthur Conan Doyle complained of how Kitchener "grew very arrogant. He had flashes of genius but was usually stupid. He could not see any use in munitions and was against tanks." General Archie Hunter had written in 1896 – before the Boer War – that Kitchener was "inhuman, heartless, vain and egotistical". Yet he was also shy, and this 6 feet 2 inches tall man had a strange propensity to sidle up to matriarchal women to be stroked! Maybe that was because he didn't spend much time with his mother during his formative years (she died when he was 14), partly because of her illness and partly because he was at various boarding schools.

Kitchener never married, and a younger man called Captain Fitzgerald was his constant companion for the last nine years of his life. Nevertheless, Pollock insists that Kitchener was not a homosexual and rejected the more probable explanation that he had homosexual inclinations but chose, like Charles Gordon, to be celibate. Nowadays most of us don't give a damn about other people's sexuality, but that was a different age, and homosexuality was illegal until 1967. Furthermore, most people would now consider that staking your son out on a lawn was a form of child abuse warranting the attention of the social services.

Statues have long been a traditional way of honouring those who are considered to be the great and the good, although at times, such as in Hitler's Germany and Saddam Hussein's Iraq, they have also been used to bolster the personality cult of leaders who were far from worthy of being honoured. They can also be the inanimate objects on which drunks sometimes urinate. There are plenty of history books where we can learn about slave traders such as Colston without honouring them. Perhaps we need to confront the past rather than let it stand, memorialised and unchallenged, in our various town centres?

However, destroying statues which somebody dislikes is the sort of action you associate with the Taliban in Afghanistan, who blew up the two Buddhas of Bamiyan in 2001. You can't erase the past simply by destroying artefacts. On the other hand, if a significant number of people are genuinely offended by the statue of a controversial person such as Colston or Kitchener, perhaps it should be removed and placed in a museum with a plaque providing details of who they were and what they did? As Kitchener was a sapper, his statue in Dock Road in Chatham would always be at home in the Royal Engineers Museum, just up the road in Gillingham.

Chapter 10

James McCudden

Steven Spielberg's 1998 film 'Saving Private Ryan' is loosely based on the true story of the Niland brothers in the USA, who were from a family of Irish descent where there were four brothers and two sisters. When it was reported that three of the brothers had been killed during World War II (two within hours of each other during the D-Day landings), the fourth was rescued from behind enemy lines and sent home to the USA. The McCudden family in Britain was Irish and likewise had four sons and two daughters, but nobody in officialdom worried about what happened to its members in the previous global conflict.

James Thomas Byford McCudden was born in Gillingham in 1895, the second son of a sergeant-major in the Royal Engineers. His father had a long career in the army, having joined as a teenager, and he eventually became an instructor at the SME in Brompton. When he left the army in 1909, the family moved to Sheerness, where James attended the garrison school and excelled at shooting and sports. However, his father's retirement meant that the family needed more income. In the year before he was old enough to enlist in the army, the young McCudden worked as a post office messenger boy. It was at this time that his interest in flying began, and he and his brothers would go from Sheerness to nearby Leysdown to watch the pioneers at the aviation centre there.

In 1910 McCudden joined the Royal Engineers as a boy bugler, spent eighteen months in Gibraltar learning about aircraft construction, and became a sapper in 1913. Shortly afterwards he was transferred to the newly-formed Royal Flying Corps to be an air mechanic at the Farnborough depot, and he soon became an accomplished engine fitter. On the outbreak of World War I in August 1914 he was sent to France, where he flew as an observer. He was promoted to corporal three months later, and in April 1915 he was made a flight-sergeant, a post which gave him responsibility for all the engines of his flight.

After McCudden had received the 'Croix de Guerre' from the French in January 1916 for his success as an observer, he was sent home to learn to fly, and he qualified at Gosport in April of that year. He flew escort for bombers, attacked observation balloons and hunted for Zeppelins. He brought down his first enemy aircraft in September 1916, and in January 1917 he received his commission. In the following month he was sent back to England, where he became an instructor, teaching about German tactics and sharing his combat experience with novice pilots. One of his students was Edward 'Mick' Mannock (1887-1918), who would become another ace pilot, and they soon became friends, partly because of their shared Irish roots and left- of-centre politics. They were sometimes looked down on by other pilots, many of whom were from public schools such as Eton and had been selected because of family connections rather than on merit.

McCudden took part in the defence of London against German daylight raids in June and July 1917, after which he returned to the frontline. He quickly established his position as the leading British pilot of World War I; his record includes shooting down 57 enemy aircraft. On 13 January 1918, he destroyed three aeroplanes in twenty minutes. His success was made on the Scout Experimental 5 machine, which is illustrated in Sappers Walk in Gillingham. Somehow McCudden found time to pen an autobiography, 'Flying Fury: Five Years in The Royal Flying Corps'. He wrote that "one cannot afford to be too sentimental when one has to do one's job of killing and going on killing", adding that "war is the most fiendish and cruel slaughter that it is possible to conceive".

Two of McCudden's brothers, William and John, had also joined the Royal Flying Corps and become fighter pilots. His older brother William was killed while flying in May 2015, while John (who James had trained) was killed in action in March 2018.

On 9 July 1918, 'Jimmy' (as McCudden was known) was promoted to major and left for France on that same day in order to take command of the famous No. 60 squadron. As he left the aerodrome at Auxi-le- Chateau on his way to the front, his engine stalled, possibly due to a faulty carburettor. He turned to land again, but his machine side-slipped into the ground in a nearby wood. He was found unconscious near the wreck, suffering from head injuries, and he died two hours later; he was 23 years old. McCudden had always been a perfectionist with his equipment, and had been known to miss meals when he wanted to align his guns and sights, which makes his death, not in action but in this way, particularly ironic.

McCudden is buried at the British war cemetery at Beauvoir-Wavans in Northern France. Just before his death, Gillingham Council had made him an honorary freeman of the town. He had received more awards for gallantry than any other airman of British nationality serving in World War I. The medals awarded to him include the Military Cross, the Distinguished Service Order and the Victoria Cross. The family name is remembered at Brompton in a group of houses known as McCudden Row.

The tragic story of the McCudden men didn't end with the conclusion of World War I. The father, who had taken a job at the Air Ministry, died in a freak railway accident at Clapham Junction in July 1920. When he stood up to offer his seat to a woman, the compartment door flew open, knocking him into the path of an oncoming train. The only surviving son, Maurice, the youngest of the McCudden brothers, had also become a pilot and served in what was by then the Royal Air Force. However, illness forced him to retire in 1933 and he died of colitis in the following year, aged just 33.

The Nilands were more fortunate. One of the three brothers who had been presumed dead survived World War II after being imprisoned in a Japanese POW camp in Burma. He died in 1984 at the age of 71. The brother who was rescued in Normandy and sent home died in 1983, aged 63.

Chapter 11

Louis Brennan

The McCudden story was mired in tragedy. The career of Louis Philip Brennan (1852-1932), who lived in Gillingham from 1883 until 1912, was dogged by bad luck.

Brennan was born in Castlebar, County Mayo in Ireland, but his family moved to Melbourne in Australia in 1861. As a child, he liked to find out how his toys worked, and when he did he tried to think of alternative uses for them. When he left school, he worked as a watchmaker, and then a few years later he was articled to Alexander Kennedy Smith (1824-1881), who was a renowned Scottish/Australian civil and mechanical engineer.

While living in Melbourne in 1874, Brennan was inspired by a cotton reel! He realised that if you tug the cotton from underneath, the reel would move in the opposite direction, and the faster the cotton was tugged the faster the reel would move. He tried to think of things that needed to move fast and not return, and he came up with the idea of a dirigible (guided) torpedo for coastal defence. He spent the next three years working on the invention, after receiving a grant of £700 from the government of the state of Victoria. He patented his torpedo in 1877 and then went back to Ireland to test the idea in County Cork.

Brennan's torpedo had two screws, revolving in opposite directions, and drums mounted on each propeller shaft were wound with wires, the ends of which were connected with a high-speed engine on shore. Steering was effected by varying the rate at which the wires were unwound from one or other of the drums by the engine, thus varying the relative speed of rotation of the screws.

When the British government heard of this invention, it saw its potential for defending harbours and channels. In 1880, Brennan was invited to come to England, where he was provided with facilities on the River Medway for the development of the weapon. The government purchased the patent for £100,000 and adopted the torpedo in 1885. That was a vast amount of money at that time, but the payment was justified on the grounds that it was important not to allow the device to pass into the hands of other countries.

In 1887, Brennan was appointed superintendent of the government factory, established at Gillingham, for manufacturing the torpedo. He held that position until 1896 and then acted as a consulting engineer until 1907. Brennan worked closely with the Royal Engineers, to whom this project was assigned, as they were responsible for Britain's shore defences at that time, and he lived at Brompton Barracks for some years before his marriage in 1892. Brennan's chief engineer at that time was John Ridley Temperley, who invented an early form of overhead crane in 1892.

The range of Brennan's missiles was limited by the length of the wire used to guide them, but they were able to reach up to two miles. They contained explosives, and the British navy used them to defend their harbours in Britain, Ireland, Hong Kong and Malta. The Brennan torpedo was the centrepiece of British coastal defence for nearly 20 years, but manufacture ceased in 1906 when shore batteries of guns with a greater range were introduced.

Brennan's next invention was a gyroscopic (which means mounted to spin rapidly about an axis and free to rotate) monorail railway system designed for military use, which he patented in 1903. It depended on the use of self-propelled vehicles travelling on a single rail, or even a tightly stretched cable, and maintained upright by a high-speed gyrostat rotating in a vacuum. He successfully demonstrated the full-sized system in Gillingham in November 1909. It attracted much attention at the Japan-British Exhibition, which was held at the White City in London between May and October 1910, and where Brennan built a mile-long monorail track and gave rides for about 40 people at a time. Some of the national press and Winston Churchill, who had recently become home secretary, showed enthusiasm for the idea, and Churchill even had a drive of the machine with some cabinet members on board. Brennan's monorail was awarded the grand prize of the exhibition.

Despite all the publicity, the monorail failed to attract government funding, and it was not developed in Britain because the railway companies had already invested so much money in the dual-rail system. Only two cars were manufactured, one of which was sold for scrap and the other was used as a local park shelter until 1930. Brennan ran very short of money, sold his luxurious five-bedroom home in Gillingham (Woodlands House) to the local council in 1912, and moved to London.

Monorails are usually either in suspended or straddled form; their major deficiency is the inability to operate in a network. However, Eugen Langen in Cologne in Germany designed an overhead suspension monorail which has been used for public transportation, covering 8.3 miles in Wuppertal, ever since 1901. Monorail building was developed in Tokyo in Japan in 1957; that was because of its minimal space requirement in a country with a severe shortage of land space and problems with traffic congestion. The Japanese have used the suspended form of the monorail over a motorway.

During World War I, Brennan was employed in the munitions inventions department of the ministry of munitions. From 1919 until 1926, he worked at the Royal Aircraft Establishment at Farnborough, where he invented a helicopter which could hover and make short flights. Its first tethered flights inside a hangar took place in 1921, and flight trials in the open started in 1924. By 1925, Brennan's helicopter had made several short lifts from the ground, could hover and could also undertake short flights, but it was seriously damaged in October of that year. In February 1926, the government decided that progress was too slow and stopped funding the project. Since the earliest practical helicopters were not introduced until 1937 by the German company Focke-Achgelis, and in 1939 by the American company Sikorsky, the British government lost an important 'first' - a helicopter which could have been used in World War II.

Undeterred, in 1926 the 74-year-old Brennan set about manufacturing a gyroscopically controlled motor car. This was completed in 1929, and it impressed several British manufacturers, particularly Morris-Austin- Rover. However, they turned it down mainly because of the high cost of changing methods, and also because they could sell all the four-wheeled cars for which they were already tooled up.

Brennan was the only one of the four men featured in Sappers Walk to marry. During the 20 years that he lived at Woodlands House, his wife developed a heart condition, so Brennan invented a stair lift for her to use. Altogether he patented 38 inventions in very diverse fields, including a silent five-key typewriter similar to those used by stenographers in law courts.

In late December 1931, Brennan was knocked down by a motor car while on holiday in Montreux, and he died three weeks later, just a few days before his 80th birthday. He was buried at St Mary's Cemetery in Kensal Green, London. In 2014, the Irish Taoiseach Enda Kenny unveiled a new gravestone for Brennan in a ceremony honouring his career.

Brennan was made a Companion of the Order of the Bath in 1892. In 1906, he became an honorary member of the Royal Engineers Institute. He was also one of the founding members of the National Academy of Ireland in 1922. In Sappers Walk, Brennan is described as 'inventor extraordinaire', but he must rank as one of the unluckiest inventors in history. Gillingham Library retains the archive of his papers.

Chapter 12

Leisure and the Military

Louis Brennan was unlucky that so many of his inventions were never taken up, but at least he could afford a holiday in Switzerland in an age when such luxuries were the preserve of the rich. The only foreign travel which less affluent men saw was when they were sent to risk life and limb in wars.

For many centuries, 'holidays' for most folk meant not having to work on Christmas Day and Good Friday, and it was not until 1871 that four bank holidays were introduced by Parliament. Throughout the second half of the 19th century, hours of work were gradually reduced, and the Shop Hours Act of 1886 restricted the employment of people under the age of 18 to a maximum of 74 hours a week. By 1900, it was usual to work for only half a day on Saturdays.

The hours of the 19th century worker seem very long now, but they did allow for more spare time than ever before. Furthermore, as working class people slowly achieved the right to vote from 1867 onwards, and after compulsory universal primary education was introduced in 1870, the demand for public facilities such as playing fields, parks and libraries started to be answered by governments. However, in an age when there were no radios and televisions at home and no cinemas in town centres, public houses were still the main 'social centres' for working men.

Almost all pubs sold only alcohol, so unscrupulous publicans would maximise their profits by aiming to send their customers away in a drunken state, and some men would drink away a large proportion of their weekly wages on a Saturday night. Soldiers, with little else to do, would frequent the numerous public houses in the Medway Towns, and inevitably some of them became involved in street rows and midnight brawls. At times the very mention of the word 'soldier' (or 'sailor') was classified with drunkenness and debauchery. It was largely that which led Hobbes (p.103), writing in 1895, to describe Chatham as "the wickedest place in the world".

The Licensing Act of 1904 reduced the excessive number of public houses with licences in congested areas such as the Medway Towns, causing something of 'a great shutdown'. Between 1905 and 1911, 7,318 premises in England and Wales were closed. When a licence was taken away, not for misconduct but for reasons of public policy, compensation was payable, not from the public purse but from a fund levied on the trade itself. This seemed fair, because the closing of some pubs increased the potential turnover and profits of those which remained.

When the Royal Engineers had first settled in Chatham in 1812, their officers had joined in the barbaric practice of hunting with the neighbouring packs of foxhounds, and they had gone shooting. They soon popularised sailing as a summer pastime, and in 1846 the Royal Engineer Boat Club was formed; its name was changed to the Royal Engineer Yacht

Club ten years later. Between 1822 and 1838, the Chatham Lines were used to hold horse-racing events.

In 1856, a regimental brass and reed band was formed, and later a string band was added, which gave a concert every Friday afternoon. Sometimes the Royal Engineers Band would stage a well-attended musical and dramatic entertainment at Rochester Theatre. During 1916 and 1917, it toured France and Belgium, giving over 150 concerts during a journey of 1,800 miles. The band continued its tour of Europe after the end of World War I. It performed at the funeral of George V in 1936, and at the coronations of both George VI in 1937 and Elizabeth II in 1953. It also performed during the opening ceremonies of the Queen Elizabeth II Bridge in 1991 and the Channel Tunnel in 1994.

By the late 19th century, London and many provincial towns had theatres and concert halls, and a popular entertainment was an evening at the music hall, laughing at the comedians and joining in the songs. The Royal Engineers provided a certain amount of musical and theatrical entertainment for the people of the Medway Towns. Some RE amateurs commenced theatrical and operatic productions in July 1860, opening with the play 'The Falls of Clyde' and the farce 'The Dead Shot'. One group of officers, known as 'The Chatham Lights', entertained quite frequently in the Medway theatres, often with the assistance of a professional lady and an orchestra consisting of members of the RE Band. From 1871, the Royal Engineer Coloured Opera Troupe provided what 'The Chatham News' (21 January 1871) described as "a new bill of fare", and which the general public could attend. They sometimes performed in civilian establishments, such as the Chatham Lecture Hall. Their programme would often be long and, according to 'The Chatham News' (27 February 1886), contained "items of an attractive character".

It was in the development of 'popular' sports after about 1850 that the Royal Engineers had their greatest impact on the leisure activities in the Medway Towns. In 1841, the Duke of Wellington issued an order that a cricket ground was to be made close to every military barracks. It is thought that cricket may have been invented during Saxon or Norman times by children living in the Weald of Kent and Sussex, but the first reference to cricket being played as an adult sport was in 1611. The first known game in which teams used 'county' names was in 1709 between Kent and London, and the laws of cricket were originally drafted in 1744. The Marylebone Cricket Club was founded at Lord's in 1787. The earliest recorded women's cricket match was played in 1745 in Surrey, and in 1864 Surrey won the first county cricket championship. The first Test Match was played between Australia and England at Melbourne in 1877.

In 1862, a Royal Engineers cricket team was established, and a pitch was constructed and fenced on the Chatham Lines in 1863. The Corps of Royal Engineers Cricket Club was officially founded in 1875. There would be occasional matches against civilian teams, such as the one-day match at Chislehurst in July 1866 against the Gentlemen of West Kent. From 1864 until 1906, two Sappers v Gunners cricket matches were played every year, one at Chatham and one at Woolwich. From 1907 it was reduced to one match a year, played at Lord's. This tradition continued until 1962, apart from during the two world wars.

In 1864, the United Services Lawn Tennis Club was started in the grounds of Fort Amherst, while the championships held by the All-England Club at Wimbledon began in 1877. The first laws of rugby were written by pupils at Rugby School in 1845, and the Rugby Football Union was formed in 1871. Two lieutenants from the Royal Engineers played for England against Scotland in the first rugby international match in March 1871, which Scotland won. The initial Royal Engineers rugby team was formed in 1886.

Ironically, to begin with only officers were allowed to take part in these 'popular' sports, but slowly the privilege was extended to other ranks. The sport for which the Royal Engineers will always be remembered in the Medway Towns is the most popular one of all, association football.

Chapter 13

When the FA Cup Went to Chatham

Football was the first mass spectator sport, capturing the enthusiasm of working people, initially in England and then gradually throughout Europe and the world. The origins of something as simple as people kicking an object around are obviously obscure, but it's known that a team game involving a ball made out of rock was played long ago by the Aztecs in Central America. On some ritual occasions, the ball would symbolise the sun and the captain of the losing team would be sacrificed to the gods.

The English version of a game resembling football was developed in the 12th century on meadows and roads, and it involved not only kicks but punches of the ball with the fist. The early forms of the game would often be played between neighbouring villages, with an unlimited number of players struggling to move an item such as an inflated animal's bladder to a particular geographical location. The matches tended to be violent, sometimes resulting in the death of participants, and so between 1314 and 1667 there were more than 30 attempts to ban football in England.

The modern version of the game developed in public schools, and for a long time there was no clear distinction between football and rugby. At Eton the ball was played exclusively with the feet, whereas at Rugby picking up the ball was allowed. Some pupils took this game with them to Cambridge University where, in 1848, an attempt was made to come up with an agreed set of rules. It was not to be. In London in 1863, the Football Association was formed, and carrying the ball was not allowed. As a result, the game divided into association football and rugby.

Football clubs have existed since the 15th century, but they weren't properly organised and had no official status. The oldest surviving football club in the world, Notts County, was formed in 1862.

The FA Cup, the oldest national football competition in the world, began in the 1871-72 season. The Royal Engineers, whose home training pitch was on the Chatham Lines, provided one of the 15 teams which entered in the first year (a record 763 teams competed in 2011-12). The very idea of such a competition provoked much opposition at the time, even from people who liked and supported football. It was argued that it would "give rise to excessive rivalry", that clubs would be tempted "to subordinate the well-being of the game to their own selfish interests", and that there would be "a lowering of the general standard of morality" among those competing.

As well as attitudes, playing conditions were very different at that time. All players were amateurs; as a result, the vast majority of football players in the 1870s were members of the leisured classes. Before 1872 the size of the ball was not fixed, and until 1875 a tape was used where the crossbar is today. At the beginning of the 1870s there were no goal nets, no free kicks and no penalties, although in 1873 free kicks for handling the ball were introduced. Until 1875 the teams would change ends every time that a goal was scored, and a throw-in was one-handed before 1882. In 1870 there were no referees or linesmen on the pitch, as it was assumed that any infringement of the laws would be purely accidental and that the two captains would settle any disputes! However, when the FA Cup competition started, it was decided that there should be two umpires, one in each half of the field, and a referee to watch over the game and reach a decision if the umpires could not agree.

The Royal Engineers reached the final in that first season of the competition, losing 1-0 to the Wanderers, which was a team from the Epping Forest area. On their way to the final, the Engineers had a walk-over when Reigate Priory withdrew, and then they defeated Hitchin, a team which was allowed into the second round despite only achieving a draw in the first round. In the third round, the Engineers beat Hampstead Heathens, and in their semi-final they defeated Crystal Palace. Both the semi-finals and the final were played at Kennington Oval; the original Wembley Stadium wasn't opened until 1923. That first final in March 1872 was watched by a crowd of nearly 2,000, who paid one shilling each for the privilege.

On the day of the final, the Engineers were 7-4 on favourites; this was therefore the first, but certainly not the last, time that the favourites were to lose a final. Gambling on big events was quite common at that time; for example, it was customary for the betting odds on the Boat Race to be published in the newspapers. A factor which contributed to the defeat of the favourites in this final was the first recorded accident in association football. Lieutenant Edmund Cresswell broke his collar bone ten minutes after the kick-off, but he stayed on the field, "maintaining his post" until the end of the game. Substitutes were not permitted until the 1965-66 season.

In 1872-73, the Royal Engineers lost 1-0 to Oxford University in the third round, but in 1874 they reached the final again, this time losing 2-0 to Oxford University. During the 1873-74 season, the Engineers carried out the first football tour in history, playing and winning matches in Sheffield, Derby and Nottingham.

1875 was the year when the FA Cup went to Chatham. 29 teams entered the competition for the 1874-75 season, and the Royal Engineers defeated Great Marlow, Cambridge University, Clapham Rovers and Oxford University on the way to the final, where their opponents were the Old Etonians. The first match resulted in a 1-1 draw after extra time. Until the year 2000, drawn finals were replayed, and the Royal Engineers won the second game, played three days after the first, by 2-0. The Engineers had become one of only seven amateur teams who were ever to win the FA Cup. A full report of both games appeared in 'The Chatham News' on 20 March 1875.

The winning Royal Engineers team in 1875 consisted only of officers – nine lieutenants and two captains. Lieutenant Sim was one of the first players to make a practice of heading the ball. Only the two players with the rank of captain had played in both the 1872 and 1874 finals as well. So much for football being a 'popular' (as in intended for the general masses) sport at that time. Maybe if the Royal Engineers had dipped into the talent pool of 'the other ranks', they might have won all three finals, but we'll never know.

Major Sir Francis Marindin had been captain of the Royal Engineers in the first two finals and would have played in 1875, but he withdrew because he was an Old Etonian and his conscience would not allow him to play against them! Verkaik (p.140) writes how "such is the intense camaraderie between boys who share the Eton experience that the bonds between them are unbreakable. They have spent five long years living together, growing up together, sharing intimate personal details and personal tragedy. They regard the school as their family." Verkaik reminds us (if we need reminding) that "Old Etonians tend to bump into each other much more than most schoolboys do in their professional lives" and "secure elevated positions". That may explain why Marindin was president of the Football Association from 1874 until 1890, and refereed the final of 1880 and all seven finals from 1884 to 1890.

In 1875-76, the Royal Engineers started their defence of the FA Cup with a 15-0 win over High Wycombe, but they were knocked out in the next round. In the following season they reached the last five in the competition, losing 1-0 to Cambridge University who, incidentally, had knocked out Rochester in the previous round. In 1878, the Engineers reached the final for the fourth and last time, only to lose 3-1 to the Wanderers, their opponents in that first final six years earlier. Surprisingly, not one member of the Engineers team in the 1878 final had played in their victorious final three years before.

1878-79 saw an early exit from the competition for the Royal Engineers, but in 1879-80 they again reached the last five out of 54 entries. For the next three seasons they reached the fourth round, defeating Reading 8-0 in the second round in 1882-83, before losing 6-2 to the Old Carthusians in the fourth round. That was their last ever appearance in the competition. However, to mark the 140th anniversary of the first final, the Royal Engineers played a match against the Wanderers at The Oval in November 2012, and the Engineers won 7-1.

After the successes of the Royal Engineers, the greatest achievements in the FA Cup by teams from the Medway Towns came from Chatham Town and Gillingham (which was founded as New Brompton Football Club in 1893). In 1888-89, when 149 teams entered the competition, Chatham reached the quarter finals, where they lost 10-1 at home to West Bromwich Albion. When there were 558 entries in the 1999-2000 season, Gillingham also made it to the quarter finals, losing 5-0 to Chelsea, the team which went on to win the cup that year.

In 1884, Preston North End was expelled from the competition because it had paid its players, but in 1885 professional football was legalised. By the late 1880s, most of the clubs who competed for the FA Cup were employing professional players. The day of amateur teams such as the Royal Engineers was clearly over.

By the 1880s, interest in football had advanced to the extent that tickets were sold for some matches. In 1888 the Football League was formed, and 12 clubs joined in the first season. Football was by now being enthusiastically supported by the working class, and it was superseding the church in the role of what Karl Marx called "the opium of the masses". Five of those founder members were clubs from mill towns, to which people had flocked in search of work after being thrown off their land by the Enclosure Acts. The competition soon expanded, requiring the Football League to have divisions, of which by 1921 there were four (the third division was divided into north and south). The Premier League was founded in 1992. The first official women's game had taken place in Inverness in 1888.

As working hours were gradually reduced, people had more time for leisure pursuits, such as watching sports like football. However, sports are not to everyone's taste, and many of the illiterate poor would contribute a halfpenny each to have stories by writers such as Charles Dickens read to them in episodes. Dickens was the greatest English novelist of the 19th century, and he spent some of the early and latter years of his life in the Medway Towns. The introduction of universal primary education in 1870 would have increased literacy, providing more people with the opportunity to read such novels for themselves.

Chapter 14

Charles Dickens

"Virtue shows quite as well in rags and patches as she does in purple and fine linen."

Charles Dickens said that in a speech in Boston in February 1842, during the first of two visits which he made to the United States during his lifetime. His novels were works of social commentary. During the Napoleonic Wars, while William Wordsworth (1770-1850) was in the Lake District writing about daffodils, not that far away small children were crawling under dangerous machinery in factories collecting fluff. A few years later, another writer with her head in the sand, produced a tedious novel lacking in substance which could be summed up in one sentence: at first Elizabeth Bennet and Fitzwilliam Darcy didn't like each other, but after a while they did. Dickens, on the other hand, wrote about the real world and was a fierce critic of the poverty and class structure of Victorian society. He campaigned vigorously for children's rights, education and other social reforms.

Dickens was born in Portsmouth in February 1812, and was the second of eight children of a clerk in the naval pay office. Because of his father's job, the family moved first to Sheerness in 1816 and then to Chatham in 1817, where they lived until May 1821 in Ordnance Terrace, opposite what is now Chatham railway station. The father, John Dickens, worked hard but rarely managed to live within his income. In 1821, the family had to move to a more modest house 'down the hill' in The Brook, and then in 1823 to London.

To supplement the family income, Charles went to work labelling bottles in a rat-infested warehouse at the age of twelve. It wasn't enough. In 1824, John was sent to a debtors' prison, where he stayed until his mother died a few months later and left him enough money to pay his creditors. Charles said that in his childhood he was happiest at Chatham, yet in an article which he wrote in 1860 he referred to the town as 'Dullborough'. His novel 'David Copperfield' is loosely based on some aspects of his own life.

During those childhood years at Chatham, Dickens would have seen hulks in the River Medway. They were sailless ships which floated but were incapable of going to sea. They provided temporary housing for felons awaiting transportation to Botany Bay in Australia. The transportees would often be working in prison gangs in the streets near Chatham Dockyard.

When he was fifteen, Charles Dickens began work in the office of a firm of attorneys, taught himself shorthand, and then became a freelance reporter. He began to report parliamentary debates, and he gained a good reputation for speed and accuracy. In 1834, he joined the staff of 'The Morning Chronicle', and the first volume of his 'Sketches by Boz' appeared in February 1836. His first novel, 'The Pickwick Papers', appeared in serial form in a magazine in 1836-37.

In 1830, Dickens had fallen in love with Maria Beadnell, the daughter of a highly successful banker. Her father thought that he was too young and lacking in prospects, so he sent Maria to Paris for a while in order to prevent a relationship from developing, although it isn't certain that Maria was particularly keen on Dickens. He based the character of Dora Spenlow in 'David Copperfield' on Maria. When he met her again over twenty years later, she was the inspiration for Flora Finching in 'Little Dorrit'.

In April 1836, Dickens married Catherine Hogarth, the daughter of another journalist, and in 1841 he travelled to the United States with his wife. He went there full of enthusiasm for the young republic, but he returned disillusioned. By 1846 he had also travelled to Italy, Switzerland and Paris. In 1858, he separated from Catherine, the mother of his ten children, and befriended a young actress named Ellen Ternan. She was his mistress for the rest of his life.

Dickens wrote novels to attack social abuses, and he made his reputation by crusading against the squalor which the Industrial Revolution had caused. Yet he himself was a creature of capitalism. He used every development, from the powerful new printing presses to the enhanced advertising revenues and the expansion of the railways, to sell his books. He tried to ensure that everyone could afford to buy his books; they were sold in cheap bindings for the poor and morocco gilt bindings for the wealthy.

Dickens therefore became rich, but he never lost his social conscience. In 1846 he founded Urania Cottage in Shepherd's Bush, which was a home for working class prostitutes, and he managed it for ten years. Dickens wrote of how one-third of babies born in London each year died before their first birthday, and he was one of the earliest benefactors of the Great Ormond Street Hospital, which opened in 1852. By 1858, the hospital was bursting at the seams and facing bankruptcy, but Dickens again provided financial help so that it would survive. The hospital features in his novel 'Our Mutual Friend'.

When he was a young boy, Dickens used to go on long walks in the Medway area with his father. He was a keen walker, and once said: "If I could not walk far and fast, I think I should just explode and perish". On one walk with his father, he saw a Georgian country house which he liked in the village of Higham, just north-west of Strood. It was called Gad's Hill Place, and Dickens was determined to buy it one day. In 1856 he did, and he used it as his main residence for the rest of his life. It was there that he completed 'Great Expectations' and 'A Tale of Two Cities', the latter being a story set in the French Revolution which, as we have seen, precipitated a chain of events resulting in the establishment of the RE Establishment at Chatham.

When the Royal Engineers demolished the medieval Rochester Bridge in 1856, to make way for a cast iron replacement, some of the rubble was recycled to build parts of Chatham Dockyard. One of the balustrades added during the Georgian period was given to Dickens, and he used it as a sundial at Gad's Hill Place.

Dickens revisited Chatham in 1860, and he was upset that his childhood home in Ordnance Terrace was, with the arrival of the railway, no longer in a rural setting; when he had lived there it was an area of fields overlooking St Mary's Church. He described it as "mysteriously gone, like my own youth", but then added "who was I that I should quarrel with the town for being changed to me, when I myself had come back, so changed, to it?" Dickens also wrote at that time of the sight and sounds of a ship being built for the first time of iron rather than wood:-

"Twelve hundred men are working at her now; twelve hundred men working on stages over her sides, over her bows, over her sterns, under her keel, between her decks, down in her hold, within her and without, crawling and creeping into the finest curves of her lines wherever it is possible for men to twist. Twelve hundred hammerers, measurers, caulkers, armourers, forgers, smiths, shipwrights; twelve hundred dingers, clashers, dongers, rattlers, clinkers, bangers, bangers, bangers!"

Rochester was Dickens' favourite town. He wrote that "its antiquities and ruins are surpassingly beautiful with lust ivy gleaming in the sun and the rich trees waving in the balmy air". He said that a visit to Rochester Cathedral was like "looking down the throat of time". Nowadays the Dickens Festival is held twice a year in Rochester, in May/June and again in December.

On 9 June 1865, there was a railway accident between Headcorn and Staplehurst in Kent, involving a train carrying 110 passengers returning from Boulogne in France. 10 people were killed and 50 were injured. Among the survivors were Dickens, Ellen Ternan and her mother. After escaping from the carriage in which they were in, Dickens assisted other passengers who were still trapped in the wreckage. However, that fact went largely unreported. In a hypocritical age when dubious relationships were tacitly accepted as long as they weren't publicised, Dickens tried to hide his involvement in the crash, in order to keep his travels with Ternan a secret.

By this time, Dickens' health was deteriorating, and he suffered a stroke in Chester in April 1869. He then stopped doing reading tours and set to work on his fifteenth novel, 'The Mystery of Edwin Drood', which he never completed. On 8 June 1870 at Gad's Hill Place, Dickens suffered another stroke and died the next day, exactly five years after that train crash. His biographer, Claire Tomalin, has suggested that Dickens was actually in Peckham when he had the second stroke, and that Ternan and her maids had him taken back to Gad's Hill so that the public would not know the truth about their relationship. Dickens had wanted to be laid to rest in Rochester Cathedral "in an inexpensive, unostentatious and strictly private matter", but he was buried in Westminster Abbey. Gad's Hill Place is now a school.

In 2002, the BBC screened a three-episode docudrama about Dickens, in which he was played by Anton Lesser. Ellen Ternan was played by Natasha Little.

Chapter 15

The Medway and the Military in Dickens' Novels

"Kent, Sir – everybody knows Kent – apples, cherries, hops and women." (Alfred Jingle in 'The Pickwick Papers', p.84)

Dickens lived in London for most of his adult life and, because of novels such as 'Oliver Twist', 'Barnaby Rudge' and 'Our Mutual Friend', he is associated in the minds of many people with the streets of the capital in Victorian England. Nevertheless, it was in the Medway area that he found inspiration for some of his greatest characters and settings. 'Great Expectations' and 'The Mystery of Edwin Drood' are sometimes referred to as 'the Medway novels'.

Rochester in particular exercised a fantastic hold on Dickens' imagination. It is used in three of his novels: under its own name as the first halting place of Mr Pickwick and his companions; anonymously as the provincial centre nearest the countryside of Pip's childhood in 'Great Expectations'; as Cloisterham, "the drowsy city", where most of 'The Mystery of Edwin Drood' is based. Rochester features in the novels of Dickens more often than any other place except London.

Eastgate House in Rochester High Street is a half-timbered building dating from the late 16th century. It is so named because it faces the east gate of Rochester Cathedral. It became Westgate House in 'The Pickwick Papers' and the Nun's House in 'The Mystery of Edwin Drood'. In the gardens of the house stands Dickens' Swiss chalet, a present from a French actor friend which arrived at Higham railway station on Christmas Eve 1864, packed in 58 boxes. Dickens used it as his study at Gad's Hill Place. Eastgate House was used as a museum of Dickens from 1923 until 2004. It is now an exhibition centre for art and history events. (There was a visitor attraction based on Dickens' works at Chatham Dockside, but that closed in 2016.)

Minor Canon Row in Rochester is a terrace of seven houses, six of which date from 1723; number 7 was added in 1735 for the cathedral organist. These elegant Georgian houses are featured in 'The Mystery of Edwin Drood', where Dickens referred to them as Minor Canon Corner. His character, the Reverend Septimus Crisparkle, a minor canon at Cloisterham Cathedral, lived in one of the houses with his widowed mother.

Restoration House in Rochester is an Elizabethan mansion which is so called because Charles II, after returning via Dover in 1660 from exile on the mainland of Europe, stayed there on the night before his ship carried him up the Thames to London to be proclaimed king, Elizabeth I had also stayed there - in 1573 on her way to Dover - and she described her accommodation as 'satis', which is Latin for 'enough'. That was the inspiration for Satis House, which was the name of Miss Havisham's rotting, cobweb-strewn home where she lived with Estella in 'Great Expectations'. The orphan nicknamed Pip referred to it "a large and dismal house". Miss Havisham was a wealthy and eccentric spinster who had been jilted at the altar and wore an old wedding dress every day of her life.

'Great Expectations' ended with Satis House being emptied and put up for sale, just as Restoration House was in the 1980s. The comedian and entertainer Rod Hull (1935-1999), who grew up on the Isle of Sheppey and became famous for his puppet called Emu, bought it for £270,000 in 1987 to prevent it from being turned into a car park. He then spent another £500,000 trying to restore it, but the cost of renovations and an unpaid tax bill resulted in his bankruptcy in 1994. He had tried and failed to sell it, because after Thatcher's government overheated the UK economy in the late 1980s, the resulting interest rates of up to 15% meant there was a housing recession. It was the first occasion in peacetime that house prices in the UK fell; between 1989 and 1995, the average property lost 12.5% of its value. In 1994, Restoration House was repossessed by Citibank and put up for sale with a guide price of £250,000. So much for the myth of Tory economic competence!

The Rochester Guildhall, a red-brick building in the High Street, was completed in 1697 and was designated a Grade 1 listed building in 1950. The council chamber featured in 'Great Expectations'. This was where, with money supplied by Miss Havisham, Pip was legally apprenticed to the blacksmith Joe. Rochester Guildhall ceased to be the seat of local government in 1974 and became the home of the Guildhall Museum in 1979.

The opening scenes of 'Great Expectations', where Pip is accosted by the escaped convict Abel Magwitch , are set in a graveyard close to Cooling marshes near Higham. The gravestones near the church porch are supposedly those of Pip's little brothers. Magwitch had been sentenced to transportation to New South Wales for life and had been imprisoned on a hulk in the Medway while awaiting his fate.

Another royal visitor to Rochester was the then Princess Victoria, who spent an uncomfortable night at the Bull Hotel in 1836. It had been built in the 16th century and was later renamed the Royal Victoria and Bull Hotel. Dickens stayed there, and it featured in 'The Pickwick Papers' and was 'The Blue Boar' of 'Great Expectations'. From here, Mr Pickwick (p.133) hired a carriage for the 15-mile drive to Dingley Dell, but the horse "drifted up the High Street in the most mysterious manner – side first, with his head to one side of the way, and his tail towards the other". (Dickens was using poetic licence there; that journey is about seven miles.)

On one winter's day when the young Dickens was going on walks in the Medway area, he skated on a pond near Cobtree Farm, close to Aylesford, and fell through the ice. The tenant, William Spong, took in the soaked Dickens, who later immortalised him in 'The Pickwick Papers' as "the hearty and hospitable" Mr Wardle, owner of the Manor Farm at Dingley Dell. That was where members of the Pickwick Society spent many happy hours.

Dickens loved the view from the medieval Rochester Bridge, which was in place until 1856. Mr Pickwick (p.129) "leant over the balustrades, contemplating nature......on either side, the banks of the Medway, covered with cornfields and pastures......rendered more beautiful by the changing shadows which passed swiftly across it, as thin and half-formed clouds skimmed away in the light of the morning sun". Mr Pickwick was not quite so impressed with the rest of the Medway Towns. He says (p.83-4) that "the streets present a lively and animated appearance, occasioned chiefly by the conviviality of the military", and that "a superficial traveller might object to the dirt, which is their leading characteristic".

When Charles Pasley, who was a great showman, first organised the demonstration of siege operations on Chatham Lines in 1833, many local people attended these ceremonies of "the utmost grandeur and importance". One of these early demonstrations is described in 'The Pickwick Papers': the manoeuvres of half a dozen regiments were inspected by the commander-in-chief; temporary fortifications had been erected, the citadel was attacked and taken, and a mine was sprung. Pasley was represented as the dashing Colonel Bulder, and he greatly impressed Mr Pickwick, who was an enthusiastic admirer of the army (p.116): "The whole population of Rochester and the adjoining towns rose from their beds at an early hour, in a state of the utmost bustle and excitement. A grand review was to take place upon Chatham Lines."

No consideration of 'The Pickwick Papers' would be complete without mentioning Sam Weller, one of Dickens' most famous characters. He is remembered for his one-liners which made fun of established clichés and proverbs, showing that they are wrong in certain situations, often when taken literally. These 'Wellerisms' include "what the devil do you want with me, as the man said when he saw a ghost", and "as you get wider, you also get wiser". Another was "I call that adding insult to injury, as the parrot said when they not only took him from his native land but made him talk in English afterwards".

Samuel Pepys, whose concern over the Dutch raid on the Medway opened this study, visited Restoration House in Rochester in June 1667. However, the last word goes to Mr Pickwick (p.83), who had a very good opinion of the military in the Medway Towns:-

"Nothing can exceed their good humour. It was but the day before my arrival that one of them had been most grossly insulted in the house of a publican. The barmaid had positively refused to draw him any more liquor; in return for which he had (merely in playfulness) drawn his bayonet and wounded the girl in the shoulder. And yet this fine fellow was the very first to go down to the house next morning, and express his readiness to overlook the matter and forget what had occurred."

Bibliography

- M.Baldwin, 'The River and the Downs: Kent's Unsung Corner', Victor Gollancz Ltd, London, 1984.

- T.Card, 'Eton Renewed', John Murray, London, 1994.

- 'Chatham News' – 12 May 1860, 13 October 1860, 14 January 1871, 20 March 1875, 27 February 1886.

- 'Chattenden and Upnor Railway', The Railway Magazine, January 1962, p. 64-5.

- W.Cobbett, 'Rural Rides', Vol 1, Dent – Everyman's Library No 638, 1966.

- R.J.Cootes, 'Britain Since 1700', Longman, London, 1968.

- E.H.Dance, 'History the Betrayer', Hutchinson, London, 1960.

- F.V.Dawes, 'Kent: A Pocket Guide', Bloomsbury Publications, London, 1990.

- D.Defoe, 'A Tour Through the Whole Island of Great Britain', Dent, London, 1927.

- C.Dickens, 'The Pickwick Papers', Penguin Books Ltd, Harmondsworth, 1972.

- 'Dictionary of National Biography',Vol 43, ed. L.Stephen, Macmillan, 1895.

- 'Dictionary of National Biography 1912-1921', ed. H.Davis & J.Weaver, Oxford University Press, 1968.

- 'Dictionary of National Biography 1931-1940', ed. L.Wickham-Legg, Oxford University Press, 1970.

- G.Green, 'The Official History of the FA Cup', Heinemann, London, 1960.

- Hansard, 11 July 1856.

- R.G.Hobbes, 'Reminiscences and Notes of Seventy Years Life, Travel and Adventure', Vol 2, Elliot Stock, London, 1895.

- J.Pollock, 'Kitchener', Vol 1, Constable, 1999

- J.Presnail, 'Chatham – the Story of a Dockyard Town and the Birthplace of the British Navy', Corporation of Chatham, 1952.

- D.Richards & A.Quick, 'Britain 1851-1945', Longmans, London, 1967.

- E.E.N.Sandeman, '150 Years of the School of Military Engineering', Royal Engineers Journal, Vol 76.

- F.F.Smith, 'A History of Rochester', C.W.Daniel, London, 1928.

- D.C.Somervell, 'Modern Britain 1870-1950', Jarrold & Sons Ltd, Norwich, 1952.

- P.F.Speed, 'Wellington's Army', Longmans, London, 1969.

- M.Swain, 'Medway FA Cup Triumph', Kent Evening Post, 10 October 1983, p.12.

- M.Swain, 'How the Sappers Got Their Name', Kent Evening Post, 24 February 1984, p.18.

- C.Tomalin, 'Charles Dickens: A Life', Penguin Press, 2011.

- N.Tomlinson, 'The Book of Gillingham', Barracuda Books Ltd, Buckingham, 1979.

- R.Verkaik, 'Posh Boys', Oneworld Publications Ltd, London, 2018.

- B.R.Ward, 'The School of Military Engineering 1812-1909', R.E. Institute, Chatham, 1909.

Online Sources

- https://en.wikipedia.org/wiki/James_McCudden
- https://en.wikipedia.org/wiki/Louis_Brennan
- https://en.wikipedia.org/wiki/River_Medway
- https://historicengland.org.uk/listing/the-list/list-entry/1005187
- https://jeremypaxman.co.uk/revelations/the-strange-death-of-lord-kitchener
- https://spartacus-educational.com/FWWkitchener.htm
- https://www.bbc.co.uk/insideout/southeast/series3/river_medway.shtml
- https://www.footballhistory.org/
- https://www.kentlive.news/news/kent-news/worst-places-live-kent-according-3555718
- https://www.kentlive.news/news/nostalgia/incredible-story-audrey-hepburn-tonbridge-2772200
- https://www.kentlive.news/news/x-rated-colourful-anecdotes-people-1193952
- https://www.kentonline.co.uk/medway/news/thousands-sign-rival-statue-petitions-228959/
- https://www.pepysdiary.com/diary/1667/06/

Lightning Source UK Ltd.
Milton Keynes UK
UKHW020907210222
398997UK00007B/221